Praise for *The Resilience Mindset*

"Resilience is a critical skill for all of us, for our careers but even more so for life. This is a must-buy book as Terry teaches how to build resilience, gain confidence, and embrace change."

—TRACEY NEWELL, board member, past president of Informatica; author of *Hers for the Taking: Your Path to the C-Suite and Beyond*

"Inspiring and practical, *The Resilience Mindset* is part memoir, part self-improvement, and weaves the author's incredible life experience into a guidebook for others to prepare and improve their lives to achieve greater happiness and purpose. This is a must-read for anyone looking to move their life forward."

—JOSEPH PUTHUSSERY, vice president of marketing, Databricks

"This is a must-read for nurses, MDs, and patients. It's inspiring, and the tools and practical exercises contained throughout will help medical professionals deal with the stressors of our occupation and impart great guidance for our patients to better handle recovery."

—MICHAEL MANN, MD, professor of surgery, Division of Cardiothoracic Surgery; director, Cardiothoracic Translational Research Laboratory, UCSF

"Storytellers like me are always on the hunt for a good redemption story. Inspired by Terry Healey's first book, *At Face Value*, I sought the wisdom and resilience presented in those pages; and now, with *The Resilience Mindset*, he offers the tools for engineering what a lot of us in Hollywood could use these days—a good comeback story."

—BILL PRUITT, five-time Emmy Award–winning executive producer of *The Amazing Race*, *The Apprentice*, and *Deadliest Catch*

"*The Resilience Mindset* provides a road map into rebuilding yourself—body, mind, and soul—after hardships. Terry's phenomenal ReBAR framework is a fresh new take on gratitude that helps others create actionable steps to propel them forward into a healthier, more fulfilling life."

—JENNIFER A. JOHNSON, RN, author of *Nursing Intuition: How to Trust Your Gut, Save Your Sanity, and Survive Your Career*

"As a surgeon, I've seen the physical toll of illness—but this book reveals the mental and emotional path only the patient knows. More than a story of survival, it's a guide for facing adversity with mindful positivity. It invites readers to reflect, grow, and find strength in the face of life's toughest challenges."

—IVAN EL-SAYED, MD, professor, director, Center for Minimally Invasive Skull Base Surgery, Otolaryngology Head and Neck Surgery, UCSF

"Finally, a book that provides practical guidance for business professionals and everyday people to find greater success and purpose despite daily challenges. This is an important book to read, and Terry is an important speaker to hear."

—GRANT RIGGS, CEO, Riggs Distributing

"Terry writes and speaks about his life-changing adversity with great courage and honesty. By sharing his proven methodology to improve self-confidence and build resilience, Terry has created a practical approach that can apply to any of life's challenges."

—LUANNE TIERNEY, chief marketing officer, Mission Cloud; board director of Crimson Wine Group

"Too many people have excuses. Terry could have had the best one. Now he has taken learnings from his personal transformation, and success as a business leader, and written an exceptional book to help others adopt more efficient approaches to success and happiness."

—PETER JACKSON, chairman, Pakked; former CEO of Bluescape and Intraware and COO of Dataflex

"Terry Healey gives a powerful account of the obstacles he has faced in his own life. His positivity is contagious, and the guidebook he provides for readers is spot on. What a fantastic tool kit others can use to help them through their own life challenges and find renewed optimism and purpose."

—LAUREN VENTURA, head of global partner marketing,
Check Point Software Technologies

"In *The Resilience Mindset*, Terry demonstrates the power of psychosocial support and therapy in his journey to wellness. His ReBAR framework provides practical tools for those struggling with cancer, or any other adversity, and will inspire so many."

—SALLY WERNER, chief executive officer, Cancer Support Community

"Terry's survival story inspires so many people who deal with head and neck cancer and provides the critical framework and guidance to not only accept life's curveballs, but to obtain proven tools and methods to cope with cancer and find purpose for a better future."

—MARY ANN CAPUTO, executive director, Support for People
with Head and Neck Cancer (SPHNC)

"Terry teaches all of us that we can choose to build a positive mindset that allows us to become more resilient, helping us to manage change and adversity in new ways. This is a powerful book!"

—PETER ALEXANDER, chief marketing officer, Barracuda Networks, Inc.

"Terry Healey demonstrates how his devastating cancer diagnosis as a young man turned into a gift and provided him with insights to create a framework and set of principles for other people facing adversity. With a thoughtful blend of personal reflection and compelling case studies, he offers a practical, actionable roadmap for anyone striving to overcome adversity and live a more fulfilling life. This book is an essential read for those seeking strength, clarity, and purpose in the face of hardship."

—ROB TUFEL, MSW, MPH, strategic planning director,
Cancer Support Community SF Bay Area

The
Resilience
Mindset

The Resilience Mindset

HOW ADVERSITY CAN STRENGTHEN INDIVIDUALS, TEAMS, AND LEADERS

TERRY HEALEY

Published by ECW Press
665 Gerrard Street East
Toronto, Ontario, Canada M4M 1Y2
416-694-3348 / info@ecwpress.com

Editor for the Press: Jennifer Smith
Copy editor: David Marsh
Cover design: Jessica Albert

Never Surrender
Words and Music by Corey Hart
Copyright © 1985 Saphir Music
All Rights Administered by Peermusic Canada
All Rights Reserved Used by Permission
Reprinted by Permission of Hal Leonard LLC

LIBRARY AND ARCHIVES CANADA CATALOGUING
IN PUBLICATION

Title: The resilience mindset : how adversity can strengthen individuals, teams, and leaders / Terry Healey.

Names: Healey, Terry, author

Identifiers: Canadiana (print) 20250208091 | Canadiana (ebook) 20250208113

ISBN 978-1-77041-856-1 (hardcover)
ISBN 978-1-77852-509-4 (PDF)
ISBN 978-1-77852-508-7 (ePub)

Subjects: LCSH: Resilience (Personality trait) | LCSH: Life change events. | LCSH: Leadership. | LCSH: Teams in the workplace. | LCSH: Success.

Classification: LCC BF698.35.R47 H43 2025 | DDC 155.2/4—dc23

PRINTED AND BOUND IN CANADA   PRINTING: FRIESENS   5 4 3 2 1

Contents

Introduction

I was happy. It was the fall semester of 1984 and I was in my junior year at the University of California, Berkeley. I was fit, had a circle of lively friends, and was dating a young woman I had become very fond of. I felt confident in my abilities and what I could achieve. I had begun to contemplate my career options. Should I gain some solid work experience for a couple of years and then pursue law school? I was curious about this because my part-time job at a law firm in San Francisco was exposing me to the world of insurance defense and I loved the investigative aspects that were critical to the outcomes of the firm's myriad cases. I was excited about life and looking forward to the future.

Then, out of nowhere, my world drastically changed. It would never be the same again.

As hard as we try to structure our lives, set goals and objectives, and aspire to be happy, the unpredictable and unknowable happen. Some of us will experience such events as negative and difficult to manage, while others will accept change as inevitable and figure out ways to exert control over their circumstances.

If your outlook leans toward seeing setbacks as roadblocks rather than opportunities, that does not mean you cannot embrace new methods to help you learn and move forward in a positive way. My story and the stories told to me by many others demonstrate the importance of being able to shift our response to adversity from one of being overwhelmed by roadblocks and hurdles to one of embracing change and seeing opportunity in struggle.

Through telling my story, I'll share the knowledge I carry and practices I make routine every day in hopes you'll find these of value as you deal with change and win the battles you are so courageously fighting.

In Part 1: A Window on Adversity, I reflect on the nature of adversity and then relate the onset of the cancer I was diagnosed with that led to multiple facial surgeries and its life-changing implications. Much of this section is devoted to the lessons I learned about dealing with the sudden onset of trauma. And to be clear, I did not carry on my battle alone. I honor my family, friends, support communities, and the wonderful medical professionals who carried me on their shoulders.

In Part 2: Introducing ReBAR: My Resilience Framework to Defeat Adversity, I present the four phases of my adversity framework, which enabled me to build my pathway and serve as the foundation of my healing journey. These phases are reflect, build, act, and renew.

In Part 3: Limitless Possibilities, I offer seven mini-biographies of people who have beaten tremendous odds and are an inspiration for all. I encourage you to learn more about these people and take a deep dive into their stories.

I want you to not only read the book but use it as a workbook to make progress in your own life. Central to progress is our mindset, and there are questions at the end of each chapter to help you build a resilient one. I urge you to make this book a personal record of your journey to become more self-confident, strong, and courageous.

Please note that I am not a doctor, psychotherapist, or life coach. But I am someone who has overcome tremendous adversity myself and found a way to build a richer, transformative life because of it. I have studied how others overcame different types of adversity and how their success led to happiness and enduring self-confidence. Because of their battles, they found new purpose in ways they could not have imagined. So I ask you to be open to new ways to approach your challenges and to be inspired to make progress every day. Don't think of the lessons and principles in this book as advice on new practices you need to employ to change your life. Instead, think of them as a framework of gifts that make life easier, more fulfilling, and more gratifying.

Let's begin.

PART 1

A Window on Adversity

CHAPTER 1

Out of Adversity, Resilience

Adversity will come calling at different points throughout our lives, whether it's the loss of a loved one, a health issue afflicting ourselves or someone close to us, a divorce, or the failure of a business. Adversity may be defined as anything that jeopardizes our quality of life. Adversity, while often uncommon in form, is commonplace. In fact, according to a study completed by Sapien Labs, 76 percent of their respondents had experienced at least one trauma or adversity over the course of their lifetime.[1]

What matters to our well-being is how we respond to adversity. That's in essence what we will explore in this book.

I like to categorize adversity into four buckets, though in many cases it may not be exclusive to any one bucket. And some might consider certain physical adversities to be caused by mental, social, or financial challenges. Regardless, the four categories listed below encompass most of the adversities we encounter in life:

1. Physical (disease, learning disability, physical disability, accident, alcohol or drug addiction, eating disorder, anxiety, depression)

---

[1] Jennifer J. Newson, "Trauma and Adversity in the General Population," Sapien Labs, August 10, 2021, https://sapienlabs.org/mentalog/trauma-and-adversity-in-the-general-population/.

2. Mental (anxiety, depression, PTSD, alcohol or drug addiction, eating disorder)

3. Social/Emotional/Psychological (being bullied, being in an abusive relationship, sexual assault, insecurity, anxiety, depression, emotional impact of natural disasters, loss of a loved one, loss of home, breakdown of a romantic relationship, divorce or family breakdown, group dynamics that lead to dangerous peer pressure, exposure to war, racism, sexism)

4. Financial (job loss, business closure, poor investment, loss of spouse, inability to hold a job, poverty, eviction from your home, impact from natural disasters)

While you may have the impression that adversity is something obvious, it may be hidden and come to light much later. Let me explain.

Many of us think the word *adversity* implies something major, and often we don't think of the little things that are happening today or are from our past that add up and, unbeknownst to us, derail us in some way that is affecting our confidence and self-esteem many years later. According to the *American Heritage Unabridged Dictionary of the English Language* as well as *Collins English Dictionary*, the word *adversity* is a noun meaning misfortune, hardship, distress, or calamity.

The "little things" and past adversities that we may have just accepted as part of life because we were too young to know better, or we failed to address them head-on because we were afraid to or didn't know how to, can often become the "big things" later in life. They can prevent us from achieving our dreams and having strong and trusting relationships. Or they can cause us so much fear that we don't have the courage to chase after certain goals because we believe we are just "not good enough." This snowball effect (little things becoming big things) is an example of how adversity can impact our self-esteem and confidence over time.

My experiences and those of others I profile are examples of how rebuilding your confidence and self-esteem is the essential building block to overcoming adversity.

True, all of us deal with adversity in our own way. Some have a hard time climbing out of the hole that adversity digs for us and realize they do not have the tools to help themselves. They seek help from friends, group therapy, or individual therapists and mental health professionals. Some who feel trapped and alone will need encouragement to get help. Some experience enormous stress from even the inconvenience of a minor misfortune like getting a flat tire, while others take major misfortune in stride, focus on what they can control, and are able to find inner strength and courage. The point is that adversity can come from a wide range of misfortunes, but how we respond determines whether we can successfully overcome our challenges. We can fall deeper into the abyss, or we can find the will and strength to climb out of it. It's about mustering courage from within. It's about making a choice each day to never indulge self-pity and self-doubt, but to fight and continue to seek the light. It's called resilience.

Learning to adapt, bouncing back, and discovering you can grow from your experience with adversity is what resilience is all about. Post-traumatic growth can give us a clearer perspective on and greater appreciation for life and spiritual development. It becomes easier to find silver linings in every adversity.

REFRAMING: THE KEY TO HOW WE LOOK AT ADVERSITY

I have always been struck and inspired by W. Mitchell's story of resilience. This courageous man suffered horrendous burns in a motorcycle accident and just four years later was paralyzed in a plane crash. In his speaking engagements he shares something I have never forgotten since I first heard it more than twenty years ago: "Before I was paralyzed there were ten thousand things I could do. Now there are nine thousand. I can either dwell on the one thousand I've lost or focus on the nine thousand I have left."[2]

As you can tell, underlying Mitchell's resilience is optimism. Research into positive thinking done by Martin Seligman (considered by many to be the father of positive psychology) at the University of Pennsylvania and outlined in his book *Learned Optimism*[3], found that individuals can cultivate a positive mindset by the way they look at setbacks. A positive mindset promotes healing and well-being, as well as recovery from adversity. The question is, how do we change the way we look at adversity? It involves reframing. Let's say we have three beliefs about setbacks: (1) whenever a bad thing happens, it is our fault; (2) everything will always go wrong; and (3) setbacks will never end. Seligman calls these the three "P's": (1) personalization, (2) pervasiveness, and (3) permanence. Reframing means we look at events as impersonal and isolated incidents, and temporary. We must do our best to learn this approach so that we can live a life with more positivity and less negativity. Here are some helpful ideas.

Accept your emotions, then move on.

We must accept responsibility where appropriate and acknowledge the new normal. Sure, initial shock, denial, anger, frustration, resentment, sadness, and grief are natural emotions that we need to allow ourselves to feel in times of adversity. Sometimes anger can be a motivating emotion and the fuel you need to start setting new goals. That's part of accepting the adversity we're experiencing. Allow yourself to have these natural emotions. Feel them. Experience them. But don't internalize them or dwell on them.

---

2   W. Mitchell, https://wmitchellspeaks.com/.

3   Martin Seligman, *Learned Optimism: How to Change Your Mind and Your Life* (New York: Vintage, 2006).

It's beneficial to reflect on your situation and make sense of what's happening, but once you've done that, leave the past behind. Don't worry about the future; focus on the present.

Facing adversity requires courage and the will to forgive.

In the struggle to overcome adversity, you will change. Your life will too. You must accept what your new life brings. That takes courage. You must also forgive others and yourself so that you can be set free from the shackles of bitterness and move on with life in a positive way. Forgiveness will do away with bitterness and resentment. Try to stop reliving whatever happened. Remember the three P's: You are not the cause of your adversity, your life will not fall apart, and the darkness the adversity has created will not last forever.

Realize that you have a choice to make—to fight or throw in the towel.

You have the power within to choose to believe in yourself and leverage that self-confidence. Choose to believe that things will start to go your way. When you make that choice, the likelihood is high they will. If you don't believe things will improve, they probably won't.

I was particularly struck by something Sheryl Sandberg said after the sudden loss of her husband during her tenure as COO of Facebook. When she and her children arrived at the cemetery for her husband's service, the children broke down. She said to them, "This is the second worst moment of our lives. We lived through the first, and we will live through this. It can only get better from here."[4] You can see how Sandberg

---

4   Sheryl Sandberg and Adam Grant, *Option B: Facing Adversity, Building Resilience, and Finding Joy* (New York: Alfred A. Knopf, 2017).

used reframing to inspire confidence and hope. These are the keys to resilience.

Many others I have talked to about overcoming adversity believe they, like Sandberg, became more empathetic because of the experience. It leads to a deeper understanding of how others feel when adversity strikes. We know what words to say to offer compassion and support. We learn through adversity to have more compassion and empathy, and to be more forgiving of ourselves and others.

FINDING PURPOSE THROUGH ADVERSITY

There are different types and degrees of adversity. Some of us deal with chronic adversity caused by trauma (for example, PTSD, depression, and anxiety), so we may feel we do not have the strength or willpower to move forward. But do not feel defeated or alone. Look to the paths that others took and use their toolkit or framework—including my own, which I will cover in part 2—to help guide your thoughts and actions. According to a study by the Substance Abuse and Mental Health Services Administration, 61 percent of men and 51 percent of women report one or more traumatic events in their lifetime.[5] In fact, 7.2 percent of American adults report experiencing a major depressive episode, 19.1 percent say they've suffered from anxiety, and 3.6 percent of Americans are living with PTSD.[6]

One thing that many people find when dealing with and working through their adversity is a newfound purpose in life that stems from helping others with similar challenges. Having a new purpose can be one of the most therapeutic parts of recovery, and

---

5   "Statistics on Mental Trauma," FHE Health, https://fherehab.com/trauma/statistics.

6   Ibid.

with purpose comes the realization that there are still lots of things we can accomplish in our lifetime despite what we may have lost.

Having a purpose may indeed be the secret to having a longer life. In his book *Be Your Future Self Now*, Dr. Benjamin Hardy shares some interesting data: "Having purpose can prolong and sustain life far beyond seemingly natural life expectancy. In the eighteenth century, the average life expectancy in America was less than forty years. Yet, most of America's founding fathers lived at least twenty years longer. Several, including Benjamin Franklin, Thomas Jefferson, and John Adams lived into their eighties. That would be like three friends living to age 110 today, when seventy-five is the current life expectancy. Purpose provides an unparalleled life force, vibrancy, and zest."[7]

A RECAP AND WHAT'S NEXT

In this chapter we looked at adversity from both a high level and a personal level. How we deal with adversity defines us; we can either be defeated or find the mental fortitude and backbone to overcome our challenges. This means reframing our story of adversity and having positivity.

In chapter 2, I'll illustrate how important it is to recognize our response to adversity so that we can bounce back and rebuild ourselves, and in many cases become stronger, more resilient, and more self-confident than we were before. We'll examine different ways adversity tests us, and especially our self-esteem. We alone control our response to our adversity; what people say and do can either lift us up or tear us down. I'll tell the story of the "take it away" guy who made an incredible difference in my recovery. The

---

7   Dr. Benjamin Hardy, *Be Your Future Self Now: The Science of Intentional Transformation* (New York: Hay House, 2022), 9.

story is my way of saying we must be alert to those who can bring us joy and caring in ways that seem like a miracle.

BUILD YOUR RESILIENCE MINDSET

Our Response Is Everything

When we are tested, it is the quality of our response that helps us understand, cope with, and see change for what it is. At the end of the day, when we're tested we discover who we are.

- What challenges are you facing today? Are there similarities between them or do they seem unrelated? How are they different? Break them down into major and minor challenges.

- Think about challenges you have faced in the past. Were you able to recover from setbacks slowly or readily? What might you have learned to deal with challenges you are facing today?

- Do you think the idea of reframing can be useful for considering new approaches to addressing your misfortune or adversity?

- What choices are you making to face adversity? Do you look outside yourself for support and resources?

CHAPTER 2

The Link Between
Adversity and Self-Esteem

W e weren't born with low self-confidence or low self-esteem. People and events chip away at our self-confidence over our lifetime, and we may not even be aware it is happening. The reason this is important is that it tells us we can find self-confidence and improve self-esteem by layering positive actions on top of one another and rebuilding what we have lost. First, let's explore why our self-confidence is tested, and why we are susceptible to doubt. Given we are all blessed with intelligence and skills to go with it, why should we ever lose confidence in what we can do and achieve?

Self-doubt happens for two reasons. An experience causes us to believe we are somehow "less than," or someone makes us feel inferior. Both lead to internalizing our self-perceived "incompetence."

Our experience may take some form of adversity—a traumatic event, painful memory, or a toxic relationship characterized by manipulation, gaslighting, or other form of abuse. It could also be that something happened to us (we went swimming and nearly drowned, we went hiking and got lost, we failed an exam, we played baseball and missed every ground ball hit to us, etc.) that made us question our ability.

We can come to doubt ourselves because someone made us question our abilities by being explicitly or implicitly critical of something we said or did. We came to believe we were somehow inadequate, incapable, or lacking in intelligence. Someone told us we looked nervous when we presented. Someone told us we weren't a gifted athlete. Someone told us we were stupid. Someone told us we lacked focus. Someone told us we would never make it as an artist. Someone told us we were weak.

Whether they questioned us or told us something they observed about us doesn't matter. If the result led us to believe we will never have an opportunity to be successful because of our shortcomings or our circumstances (we didn't graduate from high school or college; we grew up in foster care), the damage is done.

When our self-confidence declines, we begin to experience feelings of anxiety, self-doubt, and pessimism. Some of the more sensitive types among us reflect immediately on these events, while others may be able to ignore criticism and move forward because they were taught to be tough and have a hard shell. We sometimes think of these "tougher" people as less sensitive to criticism, but only those with a tough outer shell can tell us how they internalize things. Regardless of our level of sensitivity, scars begin to develop in our psyche at a young age.

These "little things" add up over time, and we aren't even aware they're changing who we are and how we feel about ourselves. For example, children who are told they need to move to a remedial class may begin to feel they are less intelligent than their class-mates. That can lead some to believe they won't ever succeed in school. Study after study shows how people who believe they will do poorly on exams tend to do poorly on exams, regardless of their preparation, because they precondition themselves to believe they are not intelligent. This negative belief leads to failure.

Believing you aren't intelligent can become a self-fulfilling prophecy as you internalize it over time. According to a psycholog-ical phenomenon known as the Pygmalion effect, low expectations lead to worse performance and high expectations lead to improved performance.[8] How do we change our mindset from having low expectations of ourselves to high expectations? How can we find an unerring belief in what we can achieve?

HOW WE FIND WAYS NOT JUST TO SURVIVE, BUT THRIVE

The wonderful thing is that all of us can find resilience, even if we doubt we have the grit and will to overcome our challenges. Time and again, I encounter people who were faced with terrible odds or consequences but somehow found a way to not just survive, but to thrive. In many cases, those who are most disadvantaged find amazing ways to continue to believe in themselves and achieve greatness. You'll read about Shawn Harper later in this book and be blown away by what he was able to achieve despite multiple learning disabilities that he was challenged with as a young man. He was bullied and ridiculed, but he was able to overcome it all. Many people look to these inspiring stories and question whether they could do the same. You can, and you will, but you have to find the courage, strength, and belief in yourself (and surround yourself with the right people) to help you get from the depths and darkness of adversity and negativity to the blue sky of opportunity and positivity.

I want you to write this next thought down: *Just as there are people who may have been critical of us in our past, there are just as many people who can inspire us to achieve greatness.* Do you remember that one teacher you had in high school who was different than the rest, who stood out to you, who inspired you, who believed in you? These people are out there, but you must be open and attentive

---

8   Robert Rosenthal and Lenore Jacobson, *Pygmalion in the Classroom: Teacher Expectation and Pupils' Intellectual Development* (New York: Holt, Rinehart and Winston, 1968).

to what people are saying to be able to take advantage of that goodness and internalize it.

Here is another thought I would like you to write down. *Remember this: we have two ears and one mouth. Listen and reflect, then act.* If you are willing to listen and open yourself up to people, and to absorb and reflect on what they say, you'll find consequential gifts to help you on your journey. Sure, you may still encounter negativity, but if you tune in to those people who exude confidence and positivity, you will find yourself moving forward. *Openness leads to hopefulness.*

Opening yourself up doesn't have to be confined to the people you know. In fact, oftentimes people we don't know can say things that we are far more apt to respond to and reflect upon, because people we know may only tell us what they think we want to hear.

In this book you will read about people I met only briefly who inspired me and made me think differently about the path I needed to take, the attitude I needed to strive for, and the drive I needed to be the person they knew (and down deep, I knew) I could become.

If you are experiencing self-doubt, you may miss the words and actions of others who can lift you up. All of us need inspiration to help us get through adversity and crisis, and the wonderful thing is that inspiration is plentiful. We just have to be open to receive these messages. One such message came to me through the "take it away" guy.

THE "TAKE IT AWAY" GUY

In 1985, I was in the hospital at UC San Francisco (UCSF) recovering from a recurrence of my fibrosarcoma cancer, which resulted in a radical maxillectomy (removal of the muscle and bone from my right cheek, the orbit and shelf of my right eye, the right half of my nose, part of my hard palate, part of my upper lip, and six of my teeth), leaving me with permanent and significant facial difference.

Because I had registered in the hospital as a Roman Catholic (I have had a strong foundation of religious faith throughout my life), volunteers visited me daily from the local parish to offer me Holy Communion. I felt that Holy Communion could contribute to my strength and courage to get through tough times because I believed in the Lord's healing power and the power of prayer.

I believed that when I swallowed the host, its life-giving properties would be carried by my bloodstream to all parts of my body to protect, to heal, and to cure. Since I had been diagnosed, I went through this visualization process every time I received the host. It always boosted my spirit and gave me more strength.

Similarly, I would bless myself upon entering and leaving church with the holy water from the font, imagining the blessed water washing impurities and any malignancy out of my tissues, and at the same time providing healing power to cure me of my disease.

About 3 p.m. one day, early in my recovery from my cancer surgery, a man knocked on my hospital room door and asked if he could come inside to say a prayer with me. Before he entered, he told me he was a volunteer at the parish down the street. "Sure, come on in," I said.

As the man entered the room, his deep blue eyes locked onto mine. His intensity didn't frighten me, but he certainly captured my attention. This was someone who clearly had a passion for helping others, and I opened myself up to him immediately. Something told me he was a gift from God.

As he approached my bed, he introduced himself to my brother Rob and my mother, who were visiting me. He said only that he was a volunteer from the church and didn't ask what I was being treated for. There was no small talk. He asked that we all join hands. He began to recite the "Our Father," and we joined him in concert. When we finished, he opened his eyes and gazed directly into mine. He squeezed my hand tightly, and his strong voice filled the room.

"Take it away! Take it away! Take it away!" He beamed and spoke with deep passion, energy, and a baritone that commanded attention. He paused and then said, "May God be with you."

He smiled, turned, and exited the room before we even had an opportunity to respond. We were dumbfounded by his intensity, and I was absorbing his kindness, his strength, and his incredible presence. I had never felt so much energy from one person in my life. For a time, no one spoke. Then I looked at my mother and Rob and said, "Wow. That was intense. I felt his power."

Up to that point in my life, I was sometimes suspicious of people and wary of their motives. But in this case, I wasn't. This was a special interaction.

As I lay in bed that night after turning out the lights, I thanked God for people like the "take it away" guy. I will never forget him. I felt like I had been plugged in and charged to full capacity, bringing me a newfound strength.

I was so taken by his energy that I decided I would one day try to track him down after I was released from the hospital and attempt to thank him for his inspiration. Was he real? Did he exist? Could I connect with him again?

I did track him down sometime later, and as you would expect, he was incredibly humble, someone who didn't need to be thanked for his ministry. Through the hospital at UCSF, I had learned he was a lector at the Catholic church right down the hill. I asked my brother Rob if he would be open to attending mass with me on a future Sunday, and he agreed. The next week, we drove out to the church.

After mass, I noticed many people wanted to talk with this angel of a person, so I awaited my turn. But he seemed in a rush, moving about the crowd. Before I knew it, I had lost sight of him. I searched in every direction and began to wonder if he was real. Suddenly, I spotted him because of his long hair. He was leaving the church grounds, walking at a brisk pace up toward the hospital. I raced up the sidewalk and was able to catch up to him, hoping my fast-paced footsteps wouldn't frighten him. As I approached him, a bit out of breath, I interrupted his brisk movement and said, "Excuse me." I quickly reintroduced myself as an ex-UCSF patient who he was kind enough to pray with. I thanked him for his words and inspiration. He acknowledged me and replied with a smile, "Good. I'm glad."

"You have a real gift," I said. "I just want you to know that I am healthy, and there are no more signs of my cancer."

"Good. I'm happy for you," he replied. He looked up the hill and quickly informed me that he was late for his next engagement. Perhaps he was headed back up to the hospital to continue his ministry for the sick.

I stood on the steep sidewalk and silently watched the "take it away" guy head farther up the hill. I reflected on who this incredible man must be. His satisfaction was not in getting thanks or appreciation. It was in doing what he was called to do. He didn't need acknowledgment. He was one of many guardian angels living on this earth.

FACING AND PROCESSING YOUR REALITY

But that follow-up encounter with the "take it away" guy was well into the future. For now, I was still in my hospital bed. I continued to reflect on my encounter with this angel of a man. He gave me the shot in the arm I needed at that time, and he provided me with the strength I knew I would need to fight. But I had to take one day at a time.

I awoke the next day and realized my plight had not changed. I was still facing a life-threatening cancer. I was still confronted with a significant facial difference at the age of twenty, a time of life when appearances matter so much.

I began to think hard about my future. It didn't help that a few social workers visited my hospital room just like the "take it away" guy did, but they had a very different approach and message. They told me I would have a long road ahead of me and that I'd need a lot of therapy. In hindsight, they were correct, but at that time, I would argue they were wrong in how they approached me. A softer, less threatening approach would likely have opened me up to considering how helpful they could be. But I hadn't even begun to process my prognosis. I hadn't even begun to understand what the treatment path ahead would look like. And at that point, pathology was still examining my tumor to determine if there were still cancer cells in my body. Was I even going to be alive in a year?

I could recover. I could survive. I could find strength. But I had to process things first, I had to reflect, I had to discover what strength and courage I could muster, and I had to convince myself that I could take this life detour to find a new path forward.

As I continued to reflect, I realized that the "take it away" guy was the thing I needed at that point in my journey to believe I would be cured. He came out of nowhere. He was an angel of healing, and his intensity and spirit gave me a newfound power. I began channeling his energy into my being whenever I began to grow concerned about a possible recurrence. I learned to employ visualization, and that became one of my key survival tactics as well.

The "take it away" guy's presence and intensity forced me to reflect on my life in a way I had never done before. I needed to allow his passion and positivity to rub off on me so I could win my fight.

A RECAP AND WHAT'S NEXT

It's tough to fight back when you're down. Losing self-esteem is a long, dark, deep descent. But adversity demands our best efforts to rally. Adversity can hit unexpectedly. Its roots might run deep because of trauma that happened some time ago. For me, it was a few cells that got sick and multiplied. I could have died. I felt that my facial difference could change my identity forever.

Finding resolve is possible. In the next chapter I relate my battle. I felt I would never know when it might be over.

BUILD YOUR RESILIENCE MINDSET

Processing Means Facing Reality in the Eye

I had been living life on Easy Street, and reflection was not part of my muscle memory yet. But now I was facing roadwork on Easy Street. From that point, I knew I had to make reflection a regular practice if I was going to conquer my enemy—the affront to my identity and very being.

- How would you rate your level of self-esteem?

- For what reasons does your self-esteem get depleted?

- In what ways do you think you are being unfair to yourself by believing you are somehow "less than"?

- Is there a "take it away" guy—someone you trust to open up to—who can lift you up?

CHAPTER 3

Detour on Easy Street

I graduated high school in Walnut Creek, California, in 1982. I was proud of the fact that I had managed to work twenty to twenty-five hours a week to save up for college—UC Berkeley—all the while maintaining an excellent grade average and competing in sports year-round. I never felt I was taking on too much and never experienced stress. I liked to be busy. I'd be grateful for these qualities later on, when I was sick and trying to heal.

The first inkling that I was unwell came from my brother Steve. Steve came over to the fraternity house to join me in attending a UC Berkeley (aka Cal) football game. He was a Cal graduate and had been a member of the same fraternity I was in. Cal was hosting its old nemesis, USC. Cal typically struggled to have winning seasons while in the Pac-12 Conference. Whenever Cal played USC—a team that seemed to rank in the top 10 season after season—we had to get fired up and believe that Cal could somehow pull off a big upset.

I used to carry out a ritual before the Cal home games and was especially excited on this nice fall day in October 1984—the sun was shining, the leaves were changing color, and a crispness was in the air. As fraternity president, I had a responsibility to do a "meet and greet" with parents and alumni, which I did as people entered the house from Bancroft Way. Then I went up to my room on the second floor, slid open the large bedroom window that overlooked the courtyard where parents and alumni gathered for drinks before the games, and played the Cal Marching Band album as loud as my 17-watt stereo and speakers would allow. Then I yelled over the music and out my window, "The Bears are gonna win today!"

But just as the music started, I heard loud knocking followed by pounding on my door. I turned down the music and walked across the room to open the door. Steve hollered "Hello" and bounced into the room. As I greeted him, he peered at me in a curious way and said, "Hey! What happened to your nose? It looks like your right nostril is all flared out."

"What?" I walked over to the mirror that hung above the sink in my bedroom for a closer look. "What are you talking about, Steve? I don't see anything." I have always taken pride in how I looked, so I brushed it off. "Let's go downstairs and grab a gin fizz," I said. Steve didn't press me and we headed downstairs to the bar.

About a week later, I was sitting on the bed in my room after dinner with my close friend and roommate, John. He was sitting on the couch drinking a cold beer and enjoying a dip of Copenhagen chewing tobacco while we chatted about our evening plans—typically what beer joint we'd meet up at around 10 p.m.

"Hey, Heals," he said, using the nickname that had also served my two older brothers in the fraternity. "I don't mean to be rude, but I've been noticing something odd about your nose. Is everything okay?"

Not again, I thought. "Yeah," I replied, feeling a bit defensive. "Everything's fine, I'm sure."

I couldn't brush off the next observation so easily. The university had recently introduced photo ID cards for students, and I had to go to the Cal administration building at Sproul Hall to pick up my new one. When I reached the front of the "H" line, the lady who managed it was quick to retrieve my card and hand it to me. She asked me to verify the information on the card and, when I glanced down at it, I wasn't looking at the print. I had to do a double take at the picture on the card, because suddenly I realized that the right side of my nose looked very distorted. I couldn't believe I hadn't noticed before on any given morning when I brushed my teeth or shaved. I touched my nose and cheek and felt a small mass that was pushing against my right nostril. It didn't hurt or feel strange in any way, so I figured it couldn't be anything too serious.

I booked an appointment to see my dentist a couple of days later. He performed a quick oral exam and took X-rays of my mouth. He suggested I make an appointment to go see an Ear, Nose and Throat (ENT) doctor in Oakland to whom he referred patients. I set up the appointment with the ENT, and a week or so later I left the Berkeley campus in my 1963 Ford Falcon to meet the doctor.

The consultation was not at all what I had expected. In some ways, it was a relief, but my intuition told me something was wrong. The doctor's comments were somewhat humiliating, because he smiled condescendingly at me after examining my nostrils and mouth and quickly pronounced that the "lump" was likely just a pimple.

I was twenty years old at this time and had had plenty of pimples. I was pretty sure this wasn't one, but I wasn't thinking of anything sinister that it might be instead. And I wasn't about to question the doctor. At that age, I was mostly apt to believe what doctors said. He suggested I use hot compresses three times a day for three weeks and come back and see him in a month if the lump was still there.

Four weeks later, I was back in his office with what appeared to be the same flaring I had begun to get used to. He thought perhaps it was a cyst or benign tumor and decided we should schedule a biopsy to rule out a malignant growth.

I left the doctor's office a little pensively, but by the time I returned to the fraternity house, I had mostly focused my mind on the positive and wasn't concerned about any malignancy. I went about my afternoon and evening as usual, and when I climbed into bed, I prayed and visualized the procedure and pathology coming back negative. I was grateful that I had a strong faith, a positive frame of mind, and an ability to combine prayer with visualization, something I picked up in high school as part of how I prepared for exams, cross-country and track races, and basketball games.

A week or so later, I had a surgical procedure to remove the "cyst" and then waited for the results. The doctor reaffirmed that he wasn't concerned, but that pathology might take a few days. In my case, one week went by, then two weeks, then three, and still I had no pathology results or diagnosis. I continued to pray and practice visualization, but I also began to get anxious and started to wonder whether I might have some form of cancer. I had been raised to always hope for the best but prepare for the worst, so I was now focused on the latter part of this life philosophy.

Finally, five weeks after the surgery, I got a call from the ENT office to come to the clinic the following day. Why did I need to visit the doctor the next day? *Tell me now!* I thought. But not being assertive, I allowed the ENT office to control the communication.

The next day, I was sitting in front of my doctor, trying to read his expression.

"Your tumor's malignant," he said. "It's a fibrosarcoma. But since we caught it in the early stages, it's unlikely that you'll have to worry about a recurrence." As I was to learn later when I researched my condition, sarcomas represent less than one-half of one percent of all cancers, and my type of sarcoma was a very rare form of sarcoma itself. It's typically found in the extremities—in the arms or legs—and rarely ever in the head and neck region. This was one of the main reasons the pathology took so long to diagnose my case. It had to be confirmed that this was indeed a fibrosarcoma. And, it was.

I was very fortunate to have received a correct diagnosis, because many sarcoma patients don't—at least not initially. And I was also blessed that I was referred to UCSF, where I met Dr. Roger Crumley, who would be overseeing my care. Dr. Crumley was an otolaryngologist (head and neck specialist) and had tremendous experience dealing with head and neck cancer, as well as surgical reconstruction. From the date of our first visit, I found him very likable, and he just seemed like a decent and honest guy. After a CT scan determined there was a mass and potentially some remaining malignancy, he suggested a follow-up procedure. The surgery was scheduled for the following week. Roughly speaking, Dr. Crumley made an incision above my gum line and along the wing of my nose to remove the remaining malignancy. It was about a four-hour procedure. I was released from the hospital the next day, with just a few sutures along the wing of my nose and a few in my palate. I felt fine and returned to my classes the following day looking like I had been in a fight with some*one*, but not some*thing*.

Life became normal again, and I was told that immediate follow-up was unnecessary. No radiation or chemotherapy. I returned to my usual twenty-year-old ways. I felt invincible. Dr. Crumley was confident they had been able to remove the tumor.

But six months later, I began to feel tingling sensations in my cheek. It felt like ants were crawling under my right cheek and upper right lip, and the tissue felt raised. I recalled my doctor saying that if I did have a recurrence, corrective surgery could result in deformity and severe scarring. Panic set in.

I went back to see my doctor, and after his examination, he believed that a recurrence was probable. I was scheduled quickly for a CT scan to confirm the return of the malignant mass, but given the potential severity of what I was facing, he also scheduled me for surgery right away too—just in case. My worst fears were coming true. My doctor decided to get me slotted into the UCSF Tumor Board schedule right away as well. The opinions of other UCSF specialists were deemed necessary. Everything happened extremely quickly. There was a tremendous sense of urgency in everything that took place.

"SO, HERE'S THE SITUATION."

My parents and my brother Rob came with me to the Tumor Board. I was examined by fifteen physicians of varying specialties, and it was anything but a calming experience. One after the other, the doctors examined my face, pushing, pressing, and prodding at my facial tissue as if it were Play-Doh. Every doctor started out by touching and pressing my right cheek where the mass was most prominent. Then each of them palpated the skin all the way up to my tear duct. I started to feel like a lifeless lab specimen, and maybe to them I was. It was striking that none of them asked questions of me. The only interaction was a brief "Hello, Terry," followed by their quick introduction—name and specialty. The doctors could have been blindfolded during their examinations of me, as they seemed to only be relying on their sense of touch. It struck me that during their brief assessments, they looked up at the ceiling as if they didn't want to hurt my feelings by looking directly at me with insincere smiles of hopefulness. I felt like I was the focus of an experiment that was being rushed because they were on a tight schedule.

Two of the doctors who examined me expressed their findings by shaking their heads back and forth. Was that the way to behave in front of a cancer patient who was becoming increasingly concerned about his survival? How could they? I will never forget the images of their two faces.

Dr. Crumley met with us after the examinations and a collaborative Tumor Board discussion that ensued. "I'm sorry for the delay," he said. "Most of the other cases today were more straightforward than yours, and most of the time was spent on your case."

My heart sank. This wasn't going to be the news I was hoping for. I felt a lump forming in my throat. Then my heart started to beat faster and faster.

"We also had some differing opinions, and that kept the discussion going on longer than usual. So, here's the situation." He paused.

"Terry, this is very serious. You may lose half of your nose, your columella—the tissue between your nostrils—half of your upper lip, and possibly your right eye."

The silence in the room was deafening. My heart began thudding so hard that I thought everyone could hear it. My mother and I stared at each other in disbelief, speechless. How could this tiny cancer have suddenly turned into a horrific, possibly disfiguring, and life-threatening disease? I was numb, like the frozen lab specimen I had felt like during the examination. I began to feel sick to my stomach.

I jumped up from my seat, ran to the door, and exited toward the restroom as fast as I could. I made it successfully into the only stall available. I began dry heaving and started to shed tears at the same time. "Oh my God. Help me, Lord."

Is my life over? Is this the end of the line for me? Can I handle what's ahead? I wasn't convinced I had it in me to undergo what lay directly ahead of me. My mind raced. My body shook. I couldn't return to the examination room with Dr. Crumley. I was an absolute mess.

The consultation was over anyway, and none of us knew what questions to ask. We were all in shock. Dr. Crumley needed to move on with his day and I couldn't face him in my current state. I needed to breathe.

STRENGTH COMES OVER THE AIRWAVES

My parents went to get the car, and Rob waited for me as I spoke to Dr. Ian Zlotolow, a maxillofacial prosthetics specialist (prosthodontist), who wanted to get an impression of my mouth before the follow-up surgical procedure so that he could build a prosthetic to fill my palate and dentures. He wanted to be sure that when I woke up, I'd be able to talk and look half human. But he didn't treat me like a lab specimen. He smiled caringly and made me feel hopeful. I am grateful he was the last doctor I saw on that day because I was able to smile as I said goodbye to him.

Finally, we were ready to go home. We had been in an examining room for over four hours. That was the first time I had smiled in all that time.

We walked out of the hospital into the cool, brisk wind and fog blowing across Parnassus Street. The Sunset District of San Francisco, where the Parnassus Heights campus stood, south of Golden Gate Park, was often shrouded in fog and cool temperatures. The air felt refreshing on my clammy face. I looked across the street, out above UCSF's Moffitt Hospital to the forested hills of eucalyptus trees, and realized once again—as I had so many months earlier during and after my first bout with cancer—that I should appreciate everything and not take anything for granted.

I might lose my right eye.

The fear struck me as I gazed at the eucalyptus trees. What would that be like? I began thinking about practical things like driving. Would the State of California even give me a driver's license if I had only one eye? How had this happened so suddenly? I had just finished my term as president of my fraternity and was at the top of my world.

And what about girls? I had always taken things like dating for granted. But suppose I ended up with only one eye and half of my nose removed, along with portions of my cheek and upper lip? I would never get another date. I'd be a total outcast.

My parents brought the car around, and Rob and I got in and buckled our seat belts. We drove in silence until we reached the freeway, about a ten-minute drive from the UCSF campus. As we began heading across the Bay Bridge, I asked my father to turn the radio on to KFOG 104.5 FM, and soon a song I hadn't heard before came on. It had a terrific beat and made me want to listen carefully. It was by a Canadian singer, Corey Hart.

> Just a little more time is all we're asking for
> 'Cause just a little more time could open closing doors
> Just a little uncertainty can bring you down
> And nobody wants to know you now
> And nobody wants to show you how
> So if you're lost and on your own
> You can never surrender

I noticed the sunshine and the blue water in the bay. I began to smile as I listened to the words.

> And if your path won't lead you home
> You can never surrender
> And when the night is cold and dark
> You can see, you can see light
> 'Cause no one can take away your right
> To fight and to never surrender

In that moment "Never Surrender" became my theme song. As we headed across Treasure Island toward Oakland, we all found ourselves smiling in the car. Corey Hart had given us a new lease on life. I felt the darkness looming over me begin to lift. Fear was being replaced by optimism and hope. I could conquer this. I could overcome whatever lay ahead.

Be aware. Be alert. Pay attention to what is happening around you. I am grateful I stayed in the moment and listened to Corey Hart's lyrics on that day.

SURGERY AND AFTERMATH

But the time came when I was once again on a gurney, waiting to see what my fate would be. The procedure lasted close to eleven hours. When I awoke in the recovery room, I was alone and began to panic. I heard no voices around me. I could barely breathe. I hurt terribly. I couldn't open my eyes. I immediately began thinking about the movie *Johnny Got His Gun*, an anti-war film about a soldier in World War I whose life is saved after he was hit by an artillery shell. Johnny is faced with true horror. He becomes doomed to live a life on a hospital bed with no sight, no sound, no arms, and no legs, but with a mind and libido as healthy as they ever were—the worst kind of imprisonment I could imagine.

I tried calling for help. Eventually, a recovery room nurse emerged to check in with me.

"What's on my eyes?" I asked, fearfully.

"Oh, that's just Duolube. It's a sterile eye-lubricating ointment. It's used to reduce the dryness in your eyes." She began blotting my eyes with a wet pad, and before I could even ask if I had lost my right eye, I felt the pressure from her fingers on my right eyeball. I was able to see her with both of my eyes.

"They saved my eyes!" I jubilantly shouted at her. I was ecstatic. Losing my eye had become my most terrifying fear.

Ultimately, the surgery resulted in the removal of half my nose, the shelf of my right eye, the muscle and bone from my right cheek, part of my upper lip, part of my hard palate, and six of my teeth. I awoke from surgery with the right side of my face literally attached to my chest and shoulder, because Dr. Crumley had transplanted a full-thickness skin graft from my chest (officially called a delto-pectoral flap) to fill in the cavity in my face.

Before surgery   Post surgery

Once I was wheeled into my room on the fourteenth floor of Long Hospital at UCSF, the nursing team tried to get me settled. Plenty of morphine, lots of dressing changes. And kindness. Each nurse was so warm, telling me how well I did during surgery, and letting me know they were there for me whenever I needed them.

I still hadn't seen what my face looked like yet. I wasn't sure I wanted to.

The morning after surgery, the nurses wanted me up and moving about, so I was given the green light to walk around a bit. I didn't hesitate. My nurse helped me out of bed, ensuring that my IV didn't get twisted around the stand as I pulled myself up. She helped me into the bathroom, but I hesitated to look at myself in the mirror. I had to muster the courage to force myself to look. I approached the mirror, but knowing I was going to be totally swollen and have sutures everywhere, I prepared myself to discount whatever I saw. This was my coping mechanism.

It was pretty much what I expected. Having touched the contours of my face and nose, and having heard from the doctors and nurses the details of the procedure, I felt the changes made to my face were as described. My nose looked as if half of it was gone. My eyes still looked symmetrical, despite my having lost the shelf of my right eye. My right lip was turned up slightly. But the delto-pectoral flap made me look like the Elephant Man.

After some cleaning up, the nurse helped me out of the bathroom, the IV stand comfortably rolling in front of me.

Once the nurse realized I was well-balanced and strong enough to move on my own, she suggested it would even be okay to walk up and down the hallways, but to be careful to always keep my IV roller ahead of me. I started my walk by turning right down the hallway, and as I got my sea legs under control, I felt a tugging on the right side of my face from the delto-pectoral flap. Because of that, I felt like I had to shuffle more than walk. I began my journey down the hallway, one short step at a time.

When I stopped looking at the floor and glanced around, I noticed that people were doing double takes at me. Some stared at me. Some even whispered as they passed me, thinking I couldn't hear them. It would take much more of this type of interaction before I realized it had started to eat away at my self-confidence.

Earlier that morning, Dr. Crumley had entered my room to check in. He was quick to point out something that would form a lasting imprint in my memory—one that fortunately was so dependent upon interpretation that it would help me slowly digest the severity of my situation.

After a quick examination, and clearly comfortable that things looked okay post-surgery, Dr. Crumley looked me in the eye and said, "Terry, I'm going to make you 'streetable' before you leave the hospital."

I asked what he meant by "streetable," but I seemed to be blocking out his answer that I'd be able to "walk the streets."

Instead, I was quickly making my own assumptions about what it meant. My mind was racing. The first thing I thought of was "acceptable." Perhaps my positivity directed my mind to acceptable rather than unacceptable. I locked in on "acceptable." Needless to say, I believed in my doctor, so why wouldn't I remain hopeful and believe "acceptable" over "unacceptable"?

My mind was working overtime though as he left my hospital room, and as I pondered the word "streetable" some more, I began to think of what real-life examples might be. I had just seen the movie *Platoon*, a Vietnam War film, which had an incredible cast that included Tom Berenger, Willem Dafoe, Charlie Sheen, and Forest Whitaker. I quicky recalled how Berenger, playing the tough guy, had this big keloid scar across his cheek from a knife wound he'd received in battle. And I thought, *Hey, maybe that's what "streetable" looks like, and if that's "streetable," that's not so bad*. I figured I could easily live with that label. In fact, a lot of girls my age probably liked that tough-guy look. Maybe it would actually pay off for me.

But I would learn later that Dr. Crumley's definition was very different than that. He was preparing me for a life of permanent facial difference. Fortunately, it took me years to realize that reality. Without knowing it, I had chosen to look at the glass as half full—probably the luckiest thing I could have done at the time. With that viewpoint, I had hope that I would eventually look like the old Terry again.

I ended up having two more procedures to remove the remaining malignancy, and by that time, my delto-pectoral flap had formed its own blood supply and could be removed. Within a couple of more days I was released from the hospital. But pathology wasn't done with me yet.

As I left the patient floor of the hospital and headed down to the main level, it became apparent that I was in a very different place. Was I just being incredibly hypersensitive, or was everyone staring at me as they walked by?

I quickly began to realize how severe my situation was, because inside the patient area of the hospital, I had felt very protected and very insulated, but outside of it, I was suddenly very vulnerable and very exposed. Did I really look that bad? I waited in the lobby for what seemed an eternity as my parents went to get the car so they could pick me up at curbside. Maybe the answer was to just hang my head down as I waited so I wouldn't have to deal with the seemingly never-ending eye-to-eye encounters.

How soon could I start reconstruction? I was beginning to realize that I needed to accelerate this process as much as possible. I was not prepared for what this stage of "streetable" was fast becoming. But I knew Dr. Crumley would get me back to the old Terry. I knew he would. I just had to be patient.

Soon, I would be informed that reconstruction couldn't start anytime soon. The margins still weren't clear from my cancer. I would need another procedure first. And now the medical team decided I would also need radiation therapy. It was going to be several months before we could even talk about reconstruction. It was another huge setback.

I ended up having about six weeks of radiation, followed by forty-eight hours of iridium seed implants that were tucked into temporary dentures in my mouth. I was cordoned off in a room on "Eleven Long" in the cancer ward, with yellow warning tape draped across my door because I was "radioactive." Only nurses and medical staff with Geiger counters to monitor me could come and go, so it was a lonely forty-eight hours. But there was one thing I could be grateful for—I wouldn't be stared at by onlookers for two days.

Afterward, I began to count the days. When could I have some form of reconstruction so I wouldn't be stared at as much? I so desperately wanted to at least blend in.

I focused on the hopeful news. My cancer had been localized, and there was no indication it had spread. The radiation was an insurance policy just in case there were any lingering cancer cells.

It was time to pause and be grateful and thankful for life. Maybe I was going to be spared. I thanked God every day.

But what became ever more difficult for me in my recovery was the aftermath of my cancer—the facial difference that resulted from it. Over the next five to six years, I had another twenty-five surgical procedures, and most of those were considered reconstructive in nature. It really took that long for me to become content with who I was as a person. But it took a series of events and turning points to get me there. That's the nature of adversity.

A RECAP AND WHAT'S NEXT

Adversity is only a detour in your life journey. That detour can be an important but temporary path that prompts you to steer a new course. Without adversity or misfortune, we sometimes find ourselves on autopilot, which can inhibit self-reflection and self-discovery. As we carry on with our day-to-day lives, we find ourselves in routines. For some, that is a preferable way of life. For others, routines instill a level of dissatisfaction and a desire for change.

When those of us looking for change decide to switch jobs or move to a new location, we feel we are in control because we have chosen a new path. This type of change is not forced on us, and we may find it exciting and typically not something we fear. It may cause some anxiety, but we generally feel more in control than when change is forced on us. In the latter situation, we must process change, and for some, it can imbue strong feelings of anger, fear, anxiety, or even sadness.

Regardless, change forces you to adapt. You can choose to think of it as an opportunity, or you can try to resist it. But resisting change never works. Change is constant in life. We must learn to embrace it or we risk further stress and anxiety.

Nature is full of adaptations. Take the jellyfish we know of today for example. Over time they learned to adapt when their early ocean movement resulted in predatory sea creatures catching and eating them as they descended toward the ocean floor. To adapt, the jellyfish began to develop new capabilities that enabled them to swim away from their predators. As a result jellyfish ruled the oceans above the sea floor for many years, and 530 million years later, they are still a very viable species,[9] even though we are now in the sixth extinction, according to many scientists.[10] And over the course of our far shorter evolution, we human beings do adapt and must adapt to survive.

Life's journey will bring us many surprises, and I look forward to someday looking back on the various detours I encountered and how they made my life richer and me far wiser. So far, I don't believe I have experienced any change that hasn't ultimately made me an improved version of myself in some way. Yes, there were setbacks along the way, but not unlike the stock market, nothing in life just moves forward along a steadily upward line. Most of the time, things zigzag up and down.

In the next chapter I will honor the people whose skills and empathy helped me through the dark times. I call them the building blocks of hope. But you also need internal fortitude. Read on.

BUILD YOUR RESILIENCE MINDSET

How to Frame Your Life's Detours

Adversity doesn't have to worsen your life. Think of it as a wake-up call and a temporary detour to help you rebuild the road you take

---

9   Netflix, *Life on Our Planet* (2023).

10   Simon Worrall, "Secret Lives of Jellyfish: Robots, Genetics, and World Domination," National Geographic, December 2, 2017, https://www.nationalgeographic.com /animals/article/jellyfish -spineless-juli-burwald.

on your life journey. Remember that detours are typically imper-
manent, and most of the time when that detour is removed, our
path is improved.

- In what ways have your hopes been dashed by adversity?
  For example, if it is a goal that has been derailed, describe
  it. Perhaps a relationship has been impacted, or your job.

- Can you recall when outsiders have inspired you to
  make changes in your life? Were they people from your
  trusted group of friends and family, or were they people
  you didn't know (like my "take it away" guy)?

- If you think back to detours you have had to take in
  your own life, how did things ultimately turn out? Are
  you grateful for them, or did they change your life for
  the worse?

- Thinking back to changes that you made in your life
  that were self-imposed, were you excited about them or
  did those changes create anxiety?

- What can you learn from your self-imposed life
  changes? Are you more resilient than you thought or
  less? Does your resilience give you confidence that you'll
  be able to confront change and adversity?

CHAPTER 4

The Building Blocks of Hope

N one of us knows from one day to the next where we're going to get the inspiration we need to change our career trajectory, to come up with our best ideas, or to get through a major crisis in our lives. We naturally look to family and friends—those whom we trust and love—but there are angels who touch us whom we do not know. In this chapter I honor those who supported me throughout my cancer treatment and its aftermath—the facial difference that resulted from it.

But know that getting through an adversity is only one part of the equation. Becoming stronger because of it, more confident, and more focused on the things that matter is what the real blessing is. We'll focus on what it takes to get through difficulty first; then, we'll move on to how you can improve your life in ways that you never imagined.

FAMILY AND FRIENDS

I attribute a lot of what kept me going from day to day to my family and friends who were there for me, regardless of their own busy schedules and the adversities they were confronting during that time. My mother, father, and brothers showed up for me each day, and the friends I knew I could count on made helping me during my recovery a priority as well. All were supportive, caring, and nurturing throughout my surgeries and the healing process.

What I remember most fondly was their positive energy. This was in sharp contrast to the very few who I thought were real friends but quickly vanished from my life. The reality that I had cancer seemed to be too much for them to handle. When I told the girl I was seeing at the time the news, she said very little and quickly distanced herself from me.

Those "friends" and relatives who couldn't bring positivity during visits with me were those I chose not to stay in touch with and not respond to when they asked if they could come for a visit or meet for coffee. I didn't feel the need to share my thoughts—that they had let me down. I didn't have the time or energy to invest in people who couldn't be supportive.

I appreciate that ridding yourself of negative people and the bad energy they put out can be difficult for people. We allow acquaintances to remain in our lives because we find it too challenging to tell them they are letting us down. These are difficult conversations and confrontations, but in times of crisis you owe it to yourself to take care of No. 1 and surround yourself only with positive energy. It made all the difference for me.

MY MEDICAL TEAM

I was blessed that I was led to the best and most kind medical professionals throughout my journey. Angels were watching over me once again. Let's categorize them into two groups—my doctors and my nurses.

My Doctors

My head and neck surgeon, Dr. Roger Crumley, was an incredibly confident and competent doctor who never expressed doubt that he'd get me cured of my cancer and reconstructed back to the old Terry. He was the definition of confidence, but not in an arrogant way. He had a charisma about him that was contagious. We all experience doubt at times in our lives, but Dr. Crumley spared me from feeling a lot of doubt because of his conviction that I was a survivor. I would have battle scars, but I would become the old Terry again. That was a powerful sentiment, and I carried it with me on my journey every day. And whether he was the surgeon to get me back to the old Terry or it was someone else, Dr. Crumley ensured that at every stage in the reconstructive process I was sent to the best and brightest of specialists. Regardless of whatever the final outcome was, trusting my doctors enabled me to keep hope throughout the process.

> Never underestimate the power of hope and what hope means in building resilience. Without hope, I wouldn't have been able to take steps forward in my journey toward an improved life.

My prosthodontist, Dr. Ian Zlotolow, was not only expert in his field but could have been a terrific sports coach or therapist if he so desired. He found ways to encourage me like no one else. One of his big mantras was talking about finding balance in life. And "Dr. Z" found his. He took up boxing when he was well into his forties, and he actually received some training from the best fighter of all time, Muhammad Ali. And during his regular workdays, he often played basketball during his lunch breaks. Despite twelve-plus-hour workdays, he made sure he found time for his outlets.

Dr. Z built many a specialized obturator/partial/palatal denture for me, and once he even created a fake nose for me to try out to alleviate my insecurities. We got to know each other pretty well on a personal level, and he would tell me about all the patients he had lost because many of them were very elderly and were being treated for basal cell carcinomas that required he build prosthetic ears, noses, and dentures. He was a people person, and losing patients was incredibly difficult for him. So, he had taught himself a lot about finding balance and outlets in life to keep him grounded.

During my radiation treatment, I was a regular in his office, needing adjustments to my palatal dentures because the radiation shrank tissue, which made the dentures tighten, causing abrasions along my gum line and palate. He would come into the examining room, where I'd be waiting to see him, and typically begin by checking in to see how I was doing so that he could observe my state of mind. One day, he noticed something different about me and said, "Hey, you seem really down today. What's going on?"

A bit defensively, I replied, "I'm just trying to take care of myself, Dr. Z. I'm trying to eat right, sleep right, and exercise." He was quick to assess my frame of mind.

"No, you got it all wrong, man," he said. "Go out with your buddies and have a few beers this weekend. You need to have some fun too."

Life is short, right? His advice was always bang on.

He knew I liked to play pickup games of basketball, so he'd always encourage me by saying, "Let's get you playing hoops again. I'm going to build you a mask you can wear with some cushion in it to protect your cheek."

He customized a mask that provided just the right support to make me feel more secure about possibly getting hit in the face. I wore it and became far more confident playing and enjoying basketball because I no longer feared that elbow to my compromised cheek and nose. He was a busy guy, but he was kind and wanted me to have more joy in my life. He never charged me for this specialized face mask. The thought of charging me for it would have never crossed his mind.

But above all else, Dr. Z helped me realize that I needed balance in my life and that I had to keep on living and doing what I enjoyed. I needed to find my own outlets that would help get my mind off the day-to-day monotony of treatment and worry and instead focus on things that gave me joy.

A Sudden Scare

As all of us know, patients undergoing cancer treatment have all kinds of side effects. I experienced an especially scary one as I entered my second week of radiation therapy, when I was back working at the law firm that had employed me for the past year or so of college.

As a legal assistant (aka a gopher), I had been immersed in one of my regular duties—photocopying case files. On that day, I was intrigued as I read the material about an accident that occurred on a Bayliner watercraft. Whenever I was doing something mundane like photocopying, I figured I owed it to myself to learn something about the case, so I would scan the material while copying.

I was in front of the copy machine, reproducing page after page of discovery material, when suddenly I noticed tears running down the right side of my cheek. I began blotting them with the sleeve of my starched, button-down shirt. For a moment, I lost focus of the legal case I was reading and began to ponder why my eye was watering so much. It hit me quickly. *Oh crap, my tumor's back*, I thought. *Could it be blocking my tear duct?*

I stopped what I was doing, packed up the files and copies, and dropped them off with the attorney assigned to the case. I explained I'd finish the copying tomorrow, which was still ahead of the deadline. I then told my supervisor I needed to get to radiation therapy early that day (a fabrication to say the least) and quickly hightailed it over to see my radiation oncologist, Dr. Ted Phillips.

I arrived well before my 3:45 p.m. daily appointment and immediately approached the receptionist. I asked her to let me see Dr. Phillips for five minutes before or after my daily procedure, because typically I only saw my radiation oncologist once a week. She said she'd find a way for me to get a visit with him that day. She was kind and always accommodating. I thanked her.

Within moments, I was ushered into Dr. Phillips's office for a quick examination. He smiled and asked what was on my mind. I filled him in on my experience that day.

He pulled up a stool across from me, removed his glasses, and did a quick examination of my entire face and a more thorough assessment of my right eye. Very quickly, he stopped and backed away from me to speak. "Terry, what's happening is that the radiation has closed off your tear duct on that side. It's nothing to worry about. I've seen this many times before with cases like yours. We'll just need to do a little procedure at some point to insert a tube in there, and it should operate just fine again."

Now, he could have said, "Maybe we should do another CT scan to make sure everything is okay." If he had said that, I would have been shaking in my boots for the next seven to ten days, anxiously awaiting my results. Instead, he told me confidently what he believed was the situation, given the time I had been receiving radiation therapy and past cases he had observed.

Quickly I calmed down. He had put me at ease. He was at the top of his profession, and because of his demeanor and vast experience, I could have peace of mind. And I am certain he was able to ease the anxiety of many other patients on a regular basis because of his certainty and professionalism.

I don't fault myself for making a mountain out of a molehill about my tear duct. Look to others who have more knowledge than you to get quick answers. Don't bottle up your fear and keep it to yourself. That approach will only foster more anxiety. Reach out to others you trust for help. More times than not, you'll be glad you did.

~~~~~~

My Nurses

I was lucky to have some of the best nurses any patient could ask for. To say they were committed to patient care and comfort is a huge understatement.

Carolyn Clary was a young oncology nurse who strived for improved patient outcomes. She had an incredibly warm smile. Carolyn was the first nurse I remember entering my private room after my transfer from the recovery room. She was engaging and confident. We had some small talk, and then she informed me it was time for my morphine shot. Soon after, she left because her night shift was over.

The next evening, she entered my room carrying a Walkman and a bunch of music cassette tapes. (Remember, this is 1985.) Knowing my age, she guessed I would appreciate some old-fashioned, classic rock 'n' roll to listen to. "For your entertainment," she said as she handed me a bundle of tapes.

Carolyn also challenged me in a way she thought might motivate me—even though we had literally just met late the night before over that morphine shot, the first I remember receiving.

My urinary catheter had been removed at some point, and I wasn't meeting the staff's requirement to empty my bladder soon enough after that. Apparently, it was Carolyn's job to change that during her shift. She entered my room carrying a very large catheter. She placed it over the end of my bed so I could see it clearly.

"What's that?" I asked.

"That's a size twenty-six catheter. That's the biggest one we've got, and that's what I'm going to use on you if you don't go to the bathroom on your own pretty soon."

I stared at the width of the tubing and gasped, realizing what this device was and where it needed to go. Carolyn crossed the room and turned on the faucet in my sink to its maximum so that I could hear it running from my bed. Frightened by what was dangling in front of me, I was able to pull myself out of bed. I walked into the bathroom with my IV stand in tow, stood over the toilet, heard the running water, and was miraculously able to urinate. It wasn't so much my fear that motivated me. It was Carolyn's devilish smile and humor. She knew how to push my buttons for immediate results.

As I reflected on that experience later, I realized she was just showing she cared and was committed to getting the best outcome for her patient, whatever that took. Call it tapping into the individual and figuring out what makes them tick, or just knowing from experience how a young male might respond, Carolyn had solutions.

One of my other nurses was Adrienne Low, who was about the same age as Carolyn. She was the definition of kind. You could tell Adrienne would never speak a negative word about anyone. She carried a warm smile with her always. One night she came into my room on her final rounds to attend to all my surgical dressings, which were numerous. I had skin grafts seemingly everywhere and dozens and dozens of staples on my chest, where the delto-pectoral flap had been returned to heal after the excision of some of its tissue to fill the cavity in my nasal area. Cleansing all these wounds was a long, arduous process, and she was very meticulous in ensuring each area was thoroughly cleaned and re-dressed as necessary.

When she finished, she walked over to the hallway door, closed it, turned off the lights, and walked back to my bedside. She pulled up a chair next to my hospital bed. She reached for my hands and asked if we could pray together, knowing from earlier conversations that my religious faith was very important to me.

"Of course," I said. I closed my eyes and listened to her soft voice.

She began the prayer, asking the Lord to give me courage and strength to heal and find peace and comfort in the days ahead. She released my hands and rose from her chair. "Thank you, Adrienne," I said. "You are very kind."

"Sleep well," she said. "Have nice dreams."

As I say to nurses to this day, "Take a risk. Be yourself and tap into patients with your intuition."

That prayer time with Adrienne was one of the most memorable and powerful experiences I had in the hospital.

> But to you, my reader, I ask that you open yourself up to people. They can and they will impact you. You have to trust that others often have your best interests at heart. We are not on this earth to find courage and strength on our own. It takes a village, and it's not just okay but a must to tap into that.

Later, after I had completed six weeks of radiation therapy, I had follow-up treatment that required I spend forty-eight hours in the cancer ward on the eleventh floor of Long Hospital. As I shared with you in chapter 3, I was cordoned off in a room with yellow warning tape across my door because I was radioactive, and I could only be visited by medical staff with Geiger counters.

Claire Alexander, another young nurse, was kind enough to ensure that I was comfortable in my room and had everything I needed, finding time to visit me periodically and give me something to look forward to during her shifts.

She seemed more concerned with providing patient care than worrying about her Geiger counter. That meant so much to me.

Show gratitude when you experience kindness, as I did with Claire, Adrienne, and Carolyn. Everyone wants to be appreciated, and that is a big part of why people do what they do every day, because what they do makes a difference. Fortunately, I was raised to always thank others for their kindness, and it paid off in spades in the hospital. I got the best care and attention in part because of my sincere and heartfelt appreciation.

MY OWN BEING

I didn't realize how much courage and strength I could find within, but what I found was predicated on the foundation of faith I had been brought up with. I often remembered the poem "Footprints," a religious parable, and felt blessed it remained top of mind during my lowest times.

"Footprints" is a poem that was written in 1964 by Margaret Fishback Powers, coincidentally the year I was born. The message focuses on a dream about two sets of footprints in the sand, one belonging to the writer of the poem and the other to the Lord. The dream continues and the writer notices that at the lowest and saddest times in her life, there was just one set of footprints. She questions the Lord and asks Him why He has left her when she needed Him most. The response is so incredibly powerful: The Lord replies that it was then that he carried her.

I was also taught to believe in myself, to have faith in myself, and though that became unbelievably challenging at various points in my journey, deep down I knew I would find a way to peace eventually. The strength in a higher power reminded me to always have hope, even in my darkest moments.

The powerful story of David vs. Goliath was one I always reminded myself about. No matter how much my cancer fought me, I could beat it like David beat Goliath. In his book *David and Goliath*, which was published years later, Malcolm Gladwell depicts the battle as the story of how ordinary people can confront giants, and it reminds us that with courage and faith, we can beat any giant we're confronted with.[11]

I chose to see myself as a fighter. I chose to keep a positive attitude. I surrounded myself with like-minded people, and combined with my faith, I knew I had the ingredients to win my battle.

Finding Purpose Through My First Job

After I had completed a series of facial reconstructive procedures, it became apparent that the progress and results were underwhelming at best. I somehow had an expectation that I would miraculously be reconstructed and sculpted back to the Terry of yesteryear.

Initially, the reconstruction was my primary focus—graduation from Cal and career objectives seemed to be on hold. But as the months ticked away, I found this lack of focus elsewhere began to further grate on my confidence level. I certainly wasn't socializing like the days of old due to my continued self-confidence decline, but a chance encounter with Peter Jackson at a Cal football game was the impetus I needed. As I pulled my Toyota FJ40 (FJ) onto the front lawn, an area designated for alumni at that time, I was greeted by several friends. The FJ was always an attention grabber, sort of like walking your puppy down the street.

Peter was thoughtful enough to bring me a cold beer from the keg on the front patio as he approached me. Peter was kind, but he was also the life of any party, a very charismatic guy. We chatted briefly, and then he offered me something. He suggested that I come and talk to him about a possible entry-level job at his start-up. Suddenly, my Saturday looked much brighter.

---

11   Malcolm Gladwell, *David and Goliath: Underdogs, Misfits, and the Art of Battling Giants* (New York: Back Bay Books / Little, Brown and Company, 2013).

As the day progressed, I began to feel a new level of excitement about life. I realized that what I really needed was to have another purpose beyond reconstruction, one that I felt I could control. My reconstruction seemed mostly out of my control.

After meeting with Peter the following week and consulting with my father about the job offer Peter was so gracious to quickly offer me, I eagerly jumped into my new role. It was just the medicine I needed. The company wasn't just growing—it was bursting at the seams. It wasn't hard to regularly log twelve-hour days Monday through Friday, and to sometimes come in on the weekend to catch up.

In time, I began to realize this job was a gift. Suddenly I had goals, objectives, and responsibilities. I was being asked to figure out how to build new service processes to delight customers, and for the first time, I began to feel like I was contributing to something beyond myself. For me that was the beginning of rebuilding some of the confidence I'd lost and regaining some self-esteem. I had been on a long downward spiral, and for the first time since my realization that I had a long journey ahead of me, I felt like I was starting to climb back up. I knew I still had a long way to go, but my first job helped sustain me and was one of the first tangible things in my life that I could point to as a confidence builder. It wasn't just showing up every day that gave me that boost, though. Rather, it was knowing I was making a difference and seeing progress that others in the business recognized. I had value to give to this world.

I'll expand on this in the next chapter as we cover other key turning points in my life that were right around the corner.

BUILD YOUR RESILIENCE MINDSET

Finding the Strength Within

When I found I had value to offer this world, it was a game-changer. Finding value cascades into newfound confidence, renewed enthusiasm for life, and direction because there is a purpose to be fulfilled. Having a purpose at every stage of life is important for all of us. As we struggle through adversity in our lives, having a clear purpose that inspires us every day can be the difference between thinking positively or negatively about our future. Having a purpose means we avoid having too much free time on our hands to be eaten up by our challenges. Here are some questions to reflect on for finding inner strength and building resolve.

- Are you aware of people who are bringing you positive energy? Have you considered how blessed you are to have them in your life? Remind yourself to stay close to those who bring you that energy.

- Are there people who bring you down when you talk to them? Do you feel they bring negativity into your life? Can you find the courage to let go of people who are not supportive?

- Are you able to find the right energy around you to boost your confidence and make you hopeful?

- Do you honor the professional people who are making a difference in your life?

- Do you tell your family and friends who are in your corner how much their love and support means to you? Show your appreciation.

CHAPTER 5

Turning Points and Inspiration

I couldn't be more grateful for the people and events that enabled me to keep my head up as I grappled day-to-day with how my life would turn out. Fortunately, and partially because I was open and attentive to what was happening around me, I spent a lot of time reflecting on things I heard from people I knew well and some I didn't know well. I reflected on how different events transpired, and in so doing, discovered several of them didn't just sustain me through my ordeal but liberated me.

DINA

In 1989, I was going back and forth between the Bay Area and Chicago's Lutheran General Hospital to have a series of six reconstructive procedures with Dr. Gary Burget, a nasal reconstructive surgeon who was considered among the best in the country. The single goal was to make my nose symmetrical again. Other procedures would still be necessary, but these were not his focus. It was now four years after the radical procedure and delto-pectoral flap I described earlier, and I had made very little aesthetic progress with my reconstruction up to that point. Nothing seemed markedly improved as I underwent each of the first five procedures. With the sixth procedure I was expecting something magical to happen.

When I was able to get out of my hospital bed after the procedure, I did what I always did once I was able to move about. I made my way to the bathroom feeling excited to see what the mirror would reveal about my new nose. But that day when I looked in the mirror, I didn't need a double take. I was extremely disappointed, devastated in fact, because I saw new scars on my forehead that had been created because tissue from that area had been used to reconstruct my nose. The surgeon had also flipped tissue from my right cheek to cover the scarring on the right side of my lip, causing new scars on my cheek and upper lip. I seemed to be fixated on the negatives.

Why wasn't the reconstruction working? How could I maintain hope? This doctor had written books and reported many success stories with patients who came to him without any nose to speak of at all. Looking at their pictures, most laypeople would never notice these patients had undergone nasal reconstructive surgery to begin with. They looked very close to perfect from my viewpoint. In fact, when I first met Dr. Burget, we spent four hours together, and during that time he showed me several of these successful outcomes. He showed me cases somewhat similar to mine, and the procedures he would use to improve my appearance.

But as I stared at myself in the mirror, I felt like I was taking two steps back for every step forward. How was I going to move forward? Why continue with surgery if my face only seemed to keep looking worse?

It was really at that point that I sunk to a new low. I wanted to cry, but instead drew away from the mirror and tried to quickly pull myself together. I tried to convince myself that the next procedure would do the trick and my face would look normal or even handsome. But my effort to maintain hope failed. I felt like a monster that no woman would ever find attractive. Where would I go from here? I felt drained. I didn't know how much strength and courage I had left.

The next day, I took a walk down a hallway at Lutheran General. I noticed a girl about my age walking toward me. She smiled and we stopped to introduce ourselves.

Her name was Dina. She had a knockout of a smile and looked kind. I thought she was gorgeous and loved her upbeat personality. She exuded confidence and did not hesitate to launch into conversation with me. Dina seemed to take a genuine interest in me. I did wonder why. I was baffled.

By day two, when I walked past her room, she seemed to be waiting for me. She yelled "Hello" and then began flirting in a way that seemed too good to be true. As we got more acquainted, we shared the reasons we were each in the hospital. Dina seemed unfazed when I told her about my cancer and the procedures I was going through. She was being treated for cervical cancer, but the prognosis looked promising. She was optimistic and I loved that about her.

We got to know each other more over the next several days. We ate some of our meals together. We walked the floor together. We even shared a bottle of wine together one night when a friend of hers snuck one in to her.

The day came when she was discharged from the hospital to return to her home in Chicago. We agreed to stay in touch. There seemed to be an incredible chemistry between us. Where had this angel magically come from when I had just reached a new low in my life? Footprints in the sand, remember?

In due course I headed back to the Bay Area. Dina and I began talking on the phone each night for hours on end. Quickly we made plans to see each other. As I was on the West Coast and she was in Chicago, we'd have to make a plan. During a call she suggested she make a trip to California and have me show her around San Francisco. We could also enjoy some wine tasting up in the Napa Valley.

I was so excited to show her around my city. "Of course!" I said. "When can you come?"

She took the trip a few weeks later, and our relationship became intimate. This was a significant detail because it was the first intimate relationship I'd had with anyone who didn't know me as the old Terry. Gone were the days of yesteryear when I could take dating and girlfriends for granted.

On our final afternoon in the wine country, Dina set her wine glass down on the table, looked me in the eye, and said, "Terry, you have a lot of issues that I cannot help you with, and you need constant reassurance, and I cannot give you that."

Boom! What had just happened?

I didn't know how to respond. She smiled at me, took another sip of wine, and broke the silence by thanking me for a wonderful weekend. We quickly pushed the elephant in the room out the door and never discussed her words for the rest of the weekend.

Upon reflection in the days after she went home, I realized there were lessons for me to learn from her words. What she taught me was that the scars on the inside had become far more disfiguring than the scars ever were on the outside. It really wasn't my physical appearance that was the issue—it was my person. Granted, her words were devastating in the moment, but they were also liberating in the sense that they put everything into perspective. Suddenly I began to realize that I didn't need to focus any longer on figuring out who that next wizard surgeon was going to be to fix my eye, my nose, or my lip. Instead, I had to focus on rebuilding what was inside.

To do that I had to listen and reflect. Without doing those two things, I wouldn't be receiving the gifts that would become important turning points in my life. Too often, we get defensive. We don't hear what we don't want to hear. We refuse to reflect. I ask that you do these two things regularly: Listen and reflect. It will change your life. It changed mine.

THE CANCER SUPPORT COMMUNITY

After Dina's departure, and some reflection time, I decided I would explore therapy. In hindsight, the social workers had been right and the time had come. Instead of seeking out counseling and therapy in a one-on-one environment, which I couldn't really afford at that point in my life, I began searching for a support group. I eventually stumbled across the Wellness Community (now called the Cancer Support Community) right in my own backyard. When I called to inquire about their programs, I was encouraged to show up the following Monday night for the next introductory group meeting. I was told I would be apprised of all the services and support groups available to me.

That next Monday, I attended my first meeting and felt so welcome and comfortable that I knew I was in the right place. The organization provides support services to cancer patients and the people close to them. While patients could attend weekly group meetings with other cancer survivors, their support people could attend separate groups with other caretakers to discuss challenges they were having that likely only others in their shoes could relate to. Both types of meetings were facilitated by licensed psychotherapists.

As I began attending the young adults support group meetings, I began to realize that all of us in the group were well older than our years. We shared a unique experience that very few people our age shared or could relate to. We talked about what really mattered in life. We talked about life perspectives. We talked openly about our fears. We talked about the insecurities all of us had about intimate relationships, given how our cancer seemed to make each of us less desirable in myriad ways—or so many of us thought.

I wanted to do more at the Cancer Support Community because I felt a sense of belonging. I asked if I could also facilitate the introductory group meetings (no psychotherapist was needed for these), which required I share my story and ask others to do the same if they felt comfortable. Then I would cover the programs available to each of them. Essentially, the purpose was to make them feel welcome but not put any pressure on them to participate.

Over time, as I met so many new men and women grappling with this horrible disease, I began to hear common sentiments, such as that my story was inspirational and that I should be incredibly proud of what I had endured and how I carried myself. Several told me that it put their own stories into a healthier perspective. A few mentioned their own disfigurement and scarring from cancer surgery, but recognized it was visible only to them. Some expressed gratitude for that.

"Really?" I would ask myself in silence. "My story is inspirational?" It was a wonderful feeling to know I was helping people and encouraging them in whatever way I could. That positive feedback helped me to feel more content. I had nothing to be ashamed of but everything to be proud of.

Just sharing our stories seemed to take a tremendous weight off. Being in a safe environment that encouraged you to share whatever was on your mind felt so liberating. I was able to discuss topics that I wasn't comfortable sharing with my own family and close friends. At the Cancer Support Community, I could open myself up and share my vulnerabilities. When I was at home or with my close friends, I focused on demonstrating my strength and toughness, but never my vulnerability. (As I would learn, showing vulnerability is a sign of not only courage, but also of strength and growth.) I was participating with my group because I was there to get help. It is okay to ask for help.

That new form of sharing taught me that when you do show your vulnerabilities, you'll find that others open themselves up to you with their own stories as well. And that's when we're at our best—when we are in a position to help each other by being honest and open about our feelings.

Within just months of attending group meetings and building a deep trust with the existing members and new participants who entered the picture, I could tell that my state of mind was improving. It wasn't that I had completely turned over a new leaf and was only experiencing upside in my day-to-day life—there were setbacks too—but my outlook was becoming more positive.

Upon reflection, as I was driving home from one of the weekly meetings at 9 p.m. after a twelve-hour workday, I realized I was more energized than ever. I was starting to take two steps forward for every step backward, instead of the reverse, which had seemingly become the course I was taking when reconstructive surgery was my life focus. I even met a woman in my group who would become a girlfriend for a short while. My insecurities were not a topic of discussion between us, as we had already talked about such things openly in the group setting. Sharing progress and setbacks with my new support system was making a huge difference. Onward and upward!

MY FIRST BOOK: A MEMOIR

Writing my first book, a memoir, and getting it published in 2001 was also a very liberating moment for me, and not in a way you might expect. Certainly, I was proud of the accomplishment, and proud of the fact that I had told an honest story, both with pictures and with words. The experience of writing was cathartic as well, but it was the unexpected that opened me up in a way I never would have anticipated. It was a life-changing occurrence.

In 2001, I was still insecure about another element I was left with from my surgery, and this time it wasn't on my face. I had two rows of thick keloid scarring across my chest from the delto-pectoral flap that had been placed back on my chest after a portion of the tissue had successfully gained its own blood supply on my face and nose. My medical team had used hundreds of staples to close the gap created between the flap and my existing pectoral tissue when it came time to return the tissue to its original state.

Tissue contracts when it is removed, and in my case, because it was suspended for a fourteen-day period, the contraction was far more significant than anticipated. The flap's sole purpose was to provide a blood supply to the new tissue that would take hold on my face. I was also left with a pancake-sized indentation on my shoulder from all the tissue that had been transplanted from that area to fill in the cavity the cancer had created on my face. Not only was it an indentation, but it was the color of the skin from the donor site on my thigh—very different than the color of my chest tissue. I would generally disguise most of the scarring by hanging a towel over my shoulder when I was at the gym after a workout, standing in front of the mirror shaving or heading to or from the shower.

At that point in my life, I played a lot of pickup games of basketball on the weekends. I usually played during the summer and fall months, and the temperature could get very hot in the East Bay, where I lived. It was often over 90 degrees in the late afternoon.

Because it was so hot, sometimes guys would suggest we play "skins versus shirts." Arbitrarily, but seemingly often, I would get picked to be on the skins team. But I always anticipated this, so I was prepared to push back, figuring no one would care who was on skins and who was on shirts.

"Ah, why don't you guys be skins, and we'll be shirts," I'd suggest.

Since I often only knew these guys from the playground and not beyond that, some would just look at me and say, "Whatever dude. We'll be skins then." No one really cared, nor did they think I might have something I was hiding, except maybe an insecurity about having pale skin.

It always seemed to work out for me. No one made an issue out of it. I was able to hide my scars and continue to avoid confronting this insecurity. It was one more thing I didn't want to have to explain to anyone. It had been hard enough when people asked me what happened to my face.

On the day that my first batch of books arrived from my publisher, something happened that changed my whole attitude. I remember coming home from work on a really hot summer day, and there at the front door was a box that UPS had left.

I was so excited. I opened the box in my office and removed a layer of protective cardboard. I quickly grabbed a copy and started flipping through it, unsure what I was looking for exactly. As I turned the pages, I came across the photograph that showed me lying in my hospital bed the day after the major procedure I described earlier, with my face attached to the delto-pectoral flap.

Then, it hit me. My book and my story were real and were out there for the whole world to see. I stopped flipping through the pages and looked out the window of my office. I was trying to absorb this moment.

Was I ready for this? Had I somehow pushed myself to do this without really comprehending how it would change my life? Was I pushing myself out in the open more than I'd be comfortable with? What had just happened here?

But I wasn't scared. It felt like I had taken a positive step and I enjoyed the feeling. I decided not to question it further.

That was a therapeutic moment, but it wasn't as liberating as what happened next. I was beaming. I was in a joyous state of mind. Often in that state, I'd find I wanted to get outside and go for a run if time permitted. I looked at my watch. It was early enough, and my wife Sue wasn't home yet. (I'll introduce Sue shortly.)

I went across the house to our bedroom, changed into my running gear, and headed out the back door. Our house was at the end of a private road, and our side fence backed onto the Iron Horse Trail, a recreational trail developed fifteen years prior as a replacement for an old railroad line. It had a paved path that spanned well over twenty miles, and beside the pavement was plenty of space for dirt paths on either side as well.

I went out our back gate, pulled off my shirt, tucked it in my shorts, and started running south toward Danville on the trail.

As I reached the first three-quarters of a mile, the point when I normally looked at my watch to check my speed, it hit me—I didn't have my shirt on. I hadn't run without my shirt on since before my surgery. *Oh my God!* I thought to myself, as I kept up a fast pace. *That was sixteen years ago! What am I doing?*

I soon realized that I had nothing to be ashamed of, but everything to be proud of. As I continued my run down that trail, I saw other runners, bikers, and a few strollers coming in the other direction toward me. As I ran along the trail, I felt proud of who I was. I wanted the whole world to see my scars. These were battle scars I was proud of.

As I continued down the path, I became more alert and attentive to other people's glances as they passed me. But I didn't notice anyone peering at my chest or checking me out in any way. I was just another runner on the trail.

I felt so liberated. I ran my five miles (two and a half each way), and when I finished and looked at my watch to see my key stats, I laughed to myself, thinking maybe I'd discovered a new tonic to running success.

I wish I had opened that box of books before my last 10K race, I thought. *I probably would have had a personal record and placed high in my age group.* The adrenaline was still rushing through me.

On reflection later that evening, it became apparent to me that maybe I should just let life unravel and allow things to happen naturally. *Don't question everything you do,* I told myself. *Just do it.*

In part 2 of the book I devote an entire chapter to reflection. Let me say here that reflection continues to play an important role in my life, and it can in yours too. If you feel fulfilled, take a minute to pause and consider why you feel at peace. Remember what it was that brought you joy. Remember what brought you inspiration. If you can do that, you are one step closer to overcoming your adversity and recognizing new strength and muscle that you now know is yours to keep.

MY WIFE AND HERO, SUE

There was one turning point that superseded all the others. That was meeting my wife, Sue.

Surprisingly, we met at a bar on Union Street in San Francisco. One of the last places I liked hanging out was in bars, primarily because it seemed, at my age, appearances were what mattered most when meeting new people in bars. Or so I incorrectly thought. My discomfort was obviously greater because I just wasn't comfortable with who I was. Let's be real—not everyone goes to bars focused only on meeting people they are attracted to.

Sometimes bars are just fun places to hang out with friends or to meet new ones. I was seated at a comfy neighborhood bar called Perry's with my brother Brian, having a drink, and in walked Sue and two other women. After she ended up sitting next to me, it seemed that the three of them were a little older and more mature than most in the bar. Quickly, a couple of guys walked toward us and struck up a conversation with Sue and her sister. One of the guys was suggesting they head somewhere more fun, like Earl's, which was more of a pickup bar than Perry's.

I leaned over to Sue as the two guys tried to order drinks from the bartender. "I don't think you want to go to Earl's," I said. "Maybe try Silhouette's in North Beach. It has a cooler vibe."

Why did I care? How did I know she wasn't familiar with bars in San Francisco? I was already in protective mode for this woman I didn't know. Maybe I was afraid she'd go to a pickup bar and get picked up! We began to talk briefly, and I found her to be very easygoing. I was comfortable chatting with her.

Sue agreed that Silhouette's sounded fun. She and her companions didn't live in the city, she said, but they were familiar with it and liked North Beach. Brian and I followed them there in a taxi less than five minutes after they left the bar. I thought, *What the hell am I doing?*

As we walked into Silhouette's, we saw Sue walking from the bar toward her sister and friend with two drinks in her hands. Whether she was surprised to see me again I do not know, but she yelled an enthusiastic "Hello!" across several tables and layers of people milling about.

"Hello!" Brian and I replied. We followed her toward her group.

Sue and I danced. We talked and got to know each other a little bit. We had an enjoyable night together. Never once did she ask what happened to me or my face.

We ended up having two dates together after that before the topic of what happened to me even came up. We were so busy talking about the here and now that we didn't even get into specifics of our past.

As I reflected after our second date, I realized how much that told me about Sue. She didn't seem concerned about whatever might have happened to me; she seemed to care more about who I was as a person today.

We got more serious. We dated for a couple of years. Then we bought a house together and even got a yellow Labrador retriever named Tiller. After three years of dating, we got married. Thirty years of marriage later, we're still together.

I wake up early every morning, and before I climb out of bed, I lean over to give Sue a kiss. Let's be honest, I am not the most beautiful sight in the morning. I barely have any hair, my nose is crooked, my right eye is drooped, my lip is pulled up to the right—and most mornings I don't even have my teeth in my mouth. (I take my dentures out regularly when I sleep). And I can guess that my breath is heinous too.

But Sue just leans over and kisses me back. And never once in thirty-plus years has she ever looked back at me and said, "You know, Terry, maybe you should think about getting your nose straightened just a bit, or getting your eye lifted a tad." She has never said that. She did tease me over the last ten years about going bald though. I think that was a bigger deal than my facial difference (in a kidding way, of course). But Sue just accepted me for who I was, and to this day has never asked me to change.

> There are angels in this world. Open yourself up to people you might never normally open up to. Be kind. People will be kind back more times than not. The world is full of gifts waiting to be opened. And none of us wants to walk alone. Surround yourself with the people who lift your spirit and your path to a better future will follow.

In part 2, I will outline the framework that I used to help me heal in all of the ways I needed to. I hope it will be helpful to you too.

BUILD YOUR RESILIENCE MINDSET

Listen and Reflect

We should listen and reflect more often. Too often, we just go through the motions. It doesn't mean we are unhappy. We can certainly live a fulfilling life by going to work every day and making that extra effort to be recognized and promoted, or by raising our children to be kind and generous, or by making sure dinner is prepared and everyone sits together at the table every night, or by helping the children with homework before they go to bed—and then collapsing into bed to repeat the same activities the next day. But it also doesn't hurt to reflect and change things up to keep life interesting.

I challenge you to take ten to fifteen minutes before you climb into bed each night to reflect on how your day went from the beginning to the end. Maybe it's a short walk with the dog before you brush your teeth. Maybe it's quiet time in the living room. Maybe it's right when you lie down at night and turn off the lights.

Did you learn anything today? Did you observe something new at work or at home? Were you inspired by something someone said? Did you say something you wish you hadn't? Should you apologize for what you said? What are you grateful for?

If you fail to do this simple exercise, you will often miss critical lessons, observations, and inspirations that might prove to be the most beneficial learnings you need to follow up on tomorrow and to start to act on now. That's how I recognized each of my key turning points in life, and so can you.

- Have you ever received feedback that took you by surprise and even hurt you? Was your immediate response to reject it? Or were you able to step back, reflect, and find the silver lining of learnings from that feedback?

- Have you found that by opening yourself up to others and showing your vulnerability, you come to feel more optimistic?

- As you read in this chapter, sometimes you never know when people and occurrences will impact you in ways you would never expect. How committed are you to being aware and receptive to new ideas and to people you meet for the first time? I encourage you to become more observant, attentive, and alert to what's happening around you and to the new people you meet every day. You'll be grateful for the new insights and abundant wisdom you will gain.

PART 2

Introducing ReBAR: My Resilience Framework to Defeat Adversity

CHAPTER 6

Reflect, Build, Act, Renew

A major plank in this book is that all of us will face adversity at some point in our lives and will figure out our own methods to cope with and hopefully overcome our challenges. Our experience will impart new wisdom and help us to move our lives forward so that future adversity is less challenging. Naturally, some of us will do better than others, but the odds of success are higher with the right preparation, mindset, resolve, and team to help us win.

The framework and process I use—and recommend to others who are facing adversity and its deleterious impact on their self-esteem and confidence—is ReBAR, and it's composed of four phases that will help us rebound from adversity more effectively:

- **Re**flect
- **B**uild
- **A**ct
- **R**enew

I have covered the reflect phase to some degree already, because it has been foundational throughout most of my life. I believe that reflection keeps us grounded and provides us the courage we need to make proactive changes in our lives. Reflection requires

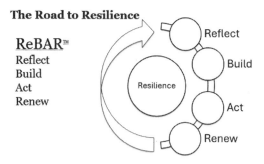

The Road to Resilience

ReBAR™
Reflect
Build
Act
Renew

Reflect
Build
Resilience
Act
Renew

quiet time to (1) rewind each day's events and consider what you may have learned that can help you be an improved version of yourself each day, and (2) express gratitude for all the blessings in your life. And sometimes we need to invest additional time in reflection to work through more complicated issues we grapple with in our lives.

The build phase requires a willingness to make changes in our lives and strive to be more flexible so that we can adapt more effectively. Reflection will guide us on our path to taking some risks that require change. Do we have the capacity for and can we be open to making changes that will improve our lives? Can we build the right mindset for success?

A key aspect of mindset is awareness. It's about being aware of how you think and behave and approaching life with positivity. Developing your mindset requires you to step back and think about what has allowed you to overcome challenges in your past to deal with present—and future—adversities. It's about creating building blocks that enable you to become the best version of yourself.

Like constructing a house, the build phase has a kind of architectural plan. It consists of a well-structured support system, trust and teamwork, a positive outlook, religious faith and gratitude, and life balance. In chapter 8 I'll go into detail for each one.

The act phase is where the rubber meets the road. It's about having goals and aspirations. It's about doing the hard work to achieve positive outcomes. This is where you begin to focus on what you can control, face challenges head-on, set goals, and consider employing therapy, visualization, meditation, and yoga in your routine so that your emotional and physical health continues to grow. You don't have to do everything at once. Set a single goal and develop an action plan for it. Perhaps starting with visualization or positive imaging will help you make progress toward that goal. Layer in other elements once you begin to find success. With each goal you achieve and each challenge you successfully address, your confidence will grow.

Be assured that these first three phases lead to finding happiness, success, and purpose. The renew phase is the commitment you make to yourself to become more resilient as you face new setbacks. There is no such thing as a straight line to success and happiness. It's a journey that requires reinforcement of the actions you take each day. It's a reminder to continually reflect, become more aware, and build upon the methods you use to cope so that new challenges become less daunting. By building muscle memory to make my framework a routine you live by each day, you will begin to feel more empowered and self-confident to tackle challenges as they emerge in your life. The renew phase is essential to success, because at this stage you are committing yourself to refreshing your steps to success and opening yourself up to continual improvement.

By practicing the four phases of my adversity framework, you will become more resilient. Resilience is what gives us the ability to rebound from life's setbacks more effectively. Resilience comes from learning to adapt, using reflection for emotional growth, and having a support system to lean on in times of need. I like to think of resilience as developing mental toughness and grit and finding your inner strength. Inner strength is something we all have, but when we're in the midst of adversity and panic, it's often more difficult to access. Sometimes we just need to step back, take some deep breaths, and dig deeper to find that inner strength. For you it might include faith, trust, and practicing self-compassion and life balance to prevent you from becoming overwhelmed with stress and anxiety. Reach out to others, pray, go for a walk, ride your bike. Do something that allows you to reset so that you can come back stronger.

BUILDING REBAR WAS TRANSFORMATIVE

I first began to construct the building blocks for ReBAR when I recognized key turning points that were occurring in my life. Allowing myself time to reflect and adapt to my life changes with a positive mindset helped me become more resilient. I began to feel I could transform myself into someone who could not only be far more adaptable and resilient in the future, but more successful in my business life and more grateful, empathetic, and kind in my personal life.

ReBAR is the life practice I use every day. By building it into my daily routine, I know I'll also be able to tap into it in the future when I need it to address another major challenge or adversity I will inevitably encounter. It's in my muscle memory now—I won't forget it, nor will I have to wait for the next adversity to figure out how best to react to the changes it requires me to make. I know I'll be able to use tried-and-true practices to recover, survive, and ultimately to thrive. The following chapters will drill down into each phase. Let's dig in.

CHAPTER 7

Phase 1: Reflect

The Road to Resilience

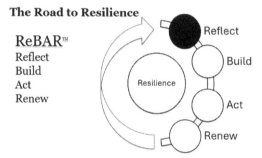

ReBAR™
Reflect
Build
Act
Renew

Resilience

Reflect

Build

Act

Renew

W hat I find magical about reflection is that the quiet time I devote to the practice frees me from the handcuffs to my laptop, daily news feeds, social media, and the constant text messages and other notifications from my mobile phone. I experience my mind opening up to my very being. In today's world, unless you live off the grid, it can be difficult to get away from all of the stimuli. But when you do escape from the noise, you will find this to be very liberating. I always look forward to the freedom of tapping into my own thoughts, uninterrupted.

Reflection enables you to find breakthrough moments that can change the trajectory of your life, but it is only possible when you make the time for it. It must become a habit that is part of your daily routine. I like to think of reflection as a baseline activity. Yes, it takes effort, but it's essential to your well-being. Don't put it off. Reflection is a discipline that helps you to navigate challenges in your personal and professional lives, especially those new and unexpected challenges that are outside your life experience.

So, how can you make reflection part of your daily life?

Personally, I look forward to taking walks with my dog, hiking in the woods, riding my mountain bike, or sitting in the backyard staring off into space, tuning in to ideas that I would never be open to while working at my desk or checking the weather for the week ahead. Don't think of this activity as a waste of time. It's anything but that. It's time you invest in yourself.

When I walk, hike, ride, or sit in the backyard, that's when I allow myself to reflect each day. If it's raining or snowing, or just too cold to be outside, I find a quiet room to sit in. As I rewind what's happening in my life and consider the challenges I'm dealing with at work or personally, often possible solutions emerge. Because I perform this activity alone and uninterrupted most of the time, I can work through how these solutions can be implemented. Sometimes I want to race home because of an epiphany I have had just walking down the street.

Sometimes our quiet time is disturbed. That's okay. We are social beings and we benefit when we collaborate and communicate with others. And sometimes meeting people on our daily walk is what provides us with new ideas and inspiration. It may not be obvious right away, but when you reflect on such conversations later, you may find a new approach to a challenge in your life. Something that's said might spark an idea. It's not always direct. It can be an interpretation of something they said that is particularly pertinent given what's on your mind at that moment.

How many times have you heard people say "I get my best ideas in the shower"? While a shower is an opportune time for reflection, it doesn't afford us enough time because we're anxious to keep to our schedule. That's why we need to allocate at least fifteen minutes to the practice every day. Some people will say they cannot possibly find fifteen minutes of quiet time during their day. I say you cannot afford not to. Reflection changed my life during a time of tremendous physical and emotional adversity.

The beauty in reflection is that we are in control of where our mind goes. No one else is telling us what to think about. We are taking the time to find nuggets, learnings, or ideas from the day's experiences that might be worth exploring later, and taking time to be grateful that we have time to reflect. Think of it as a gift or a luxury. Who doesn't want those wonderful things in their life? You'll find that reflection is not a chore in any way.

> We make choices every day and those choices dictate the direction of our lives. If I asked you to find fifteen minutes a day to reflect, could you find the time? Maybe not. But if I said to you, "If you find fifteen minutes a day to reflect, it will change your life for the better," would you then be more likely to find the time? Perhaps.

BE RECEPTIVE TO NEW IDEAS

We all have the potential to improve our lives and find that each day can be filled with excitement if we try new ideas and approaches. Trying new things might be scary for you, but most of the time we end up being glad we stepped out of the box and tried something new. It can be liberating to discover possibilities and put them into action. If something isn't working after you try it, future reflection will inform you of that too. Maybe there is another path. But if you don't take the time to reflect at all, you'll never know the possibilities you are missing out on.

Successful business, healthcare and educational leaders, athletes, musicians, actors, and other professionals don't reach their level of success because the stars just magically aligned. They faced times of failure at some stage that led them to step back and consider what they should do differently. It takes guts to be vulnerable and open yourself up to the realization that maybe your current approach isn't optimal. Maybe it isn't serving your purpose well, and if so you need to think about what might not be working, or what could be the next opportunity to try.

You don't need to feel pressure to come up with new ideas completely on your own either. Sometimes they will come from within, but sometimes they'll come from outside influences. And allow your reflections to produce new ideas at their natural pace. Sometimes it will take a month or longer. That's okay.

Be Receptive to Others' Thoughts

Be open-minded and willing to interact and listen to what other people have to say. Reflecting on comments from others, whether friends or strangers, can often be the light bulb that enables you to start thinking differently. It's critical to reflect on what is transpiring around you. I'll cover mindfulness in chapter 9, but as in mindfulness, try to live in the moment and be attuned to what you hear, smell, and see. When you begin to breathe freely and allow your mind and body to open, amazing things can happen. You relax and release. And these actions are not only calming but can even recharge you and renew you.

I am a firm believer that there are no coincidences. When you are open-minded and something happens that seems significant to the time and place you are in, or people enter your life and you feel a strong connection to them and are inspired by their words, it's worthwhile to reflect. Consider whether you might benefit by implementing that new idea or inspiration. What are the pros and cons? Remember to be aware, alert, and attentive to what's happening around you, because the people you interact with and the events that transpire can and will inspire you.

Embrace the Gifts that Others Bring You

Reflection was the lynchpin that enabled me to make leaps of progress to address my challenges and realize that I could not overcome my adversity alone. I needed the help and inspiration of others to help me heal—physically, mentally, and spiritually. I was fortunate to have such an amazing community of support. I owed it to myself and to them to ponder daily events and activities to assess what I could learn from them and how they could inspire change. We must remind ourselves that we don't have all the answers. We make choices based on our experiences and interactions that lead us to determine what path we want to take going forward.

BUILD YOUR RESILIENCE MINDSET

Putting the Reflection Phase into Practice

I can assure you that if you don't practice self-reflection, you will end up in a rut of doing the same things and acting the same way, day in and day out. This approach will stunt your personal growth and affect your well-being, as well as the well-being of your loved ones. Without self-reflection, you'll feel like problems remain unsolved—because they will remain unsolved. It's important to take time for yourself.

Doing so will keep you grounded and help with learning new things and trying new ideas. It will also allow time for constructive thinking so that you can consider how you might change an approach when you feel you have failed at something. This will help in both your personal and professional lives. Why not get started now? Can you spare fifteen minutes and then start to make your judgment about reflection?

I would argue that daily reflections are essential to your emotional stability and growth. And while reflection is a useful practice when dealing with serious adversity or minor setbacks, it is worthwhile even when you feel life is stable and settled.

Reflection can be fun, exciting, and full of possibilities, and that's why making it a part of your daily routine is essential to growth. Reflection is a discipline that will give you more clarity on your path and purpose. When we have a purpose, we are more motivated, happier, and more creative.

When you take the time to get away from life's interruptions for fifteen minutes, you can take a deep breath, clear your mind of your last phone call or email, and reflect on the big picture of what's happening in your life. Now is the time to think like the CEO of your life. What questions can you ask yourself to have better control?

Think about what you are grateful for during this exercise period, because that reinforces all the good that you have in your life, and it prevents self-pity and blame for any struggle you may be encountering. Forgiveness is important to incorporate too, especially when moving past an adversity that was caused by someone hurting you. Reflect and find the courage to forgive and let go. Forgiveness allows us to take back the power and move forward in our healing process.

There is a lot to consider here, so let's list the questions to ask ourselves each day. Feel free to choose questions that apply to your life circumstances and add them to your reflection practice. You could choose to sit outside or in a quiet room away from constant interruptions to find it easier to reflect, and could even write down your thoughts in a notebook or on your tablet.

Reflect on Highlights of the Day

- What were the big moments of the day? Did something happen that was outside of the ordinary?

- Were there positive moments? Why did they occur?

- Were you inspired by something that happened today? Why? Is there any action you can take from that?

- Did you accomplish something in your personal life today? Are you proud of that? Can you build on what you accomplished?

- Were there negative moments? Why did they occur?

- What are you struggling with today?

Reflect on Workplace Activities

- Did you make an impact at work today? Did you have an idea that warrants following up and moving forward with?

- Are you willing to be courageous and vulnerable, and step out of your comfort zone to propose that new idea? What's the worst thing that can happen?

Reflect on Outside Influences

- Were you inspired by someone today? Why? What did they say or do? Is there any action you can take from that?

- Do you feel you could have handled an encounter with someone differently to ensure a better outcome? How could you have done that? What can you learn from that experience?

- Did someone hurt you today? Can you find the courage to forgive them so you can move past the pain and heal from it? What can you learn from this? Do you need to set some new boundaries?

- Did you contribute anything noteworthy today for others to benefit from? Recognize what you did. Celebrate it. You'll feel more self-confident tomorrow.

Taking a Deep Dive into Reflection

The practice of reflection leads to deeper introspection, which is a very important asset when you need to make significant life changes. When life is no longer stable and settled—for example, when you are dissatisfied with your work or personal life, or are struggling with major life challenges—the practice of daily reflection will guide you to create the right mindset, draw from your well of resilience, and adapt with confidence to change.

My approach is not a curriculum to follow per se. Allowing yourself the freedom to reflect will help you realize if doing a deeper dive will help you. The deeper dive is a slightly different approach to improving your emotional health. When you feel you need to do more work to find peace, contentment, and positivity, consider deeper-dive reflection.

Find an hour to consider bigger-picture reflections. In this case, you will want to document your thoughts, so go outside with your laptop or tablet, go to a coffee shop, or find a quiet spot. Turn off your email and silence your phone so that you don't get distracted by text messages or phone calls.

Compared to daily reflection, deep dives can be more challenging. Consider the practice a periodic exercise to complement daily reflection. When you are at a crossroads or inflection point due to conflict or adversity, working through many key issues at one time helps to put life into perspective, develop the appropriate mindset, and build a plan to move forward.

Deep-dive reflection requires that you ask yourself a broader and deeper set of questions than those in your daily reflection. It's far more prescriptive. That said, it will give you the playbook to move forward and provide more clarity about your life path and purpose.

Reflect on Appreciation

- What are you grateful for?

- Who are you grateful for?

- What did someone say or do today that you are grateful for?

- What blessings were you raised with?

Reflect on Ways to Find Strength

- Is faith important to you? How do you benefit from faith?

- Do you have hope or do you feel hopeless? Why?

Reflect on Your Traits

- Are you willing to express your vulnerabilities and open up in front of others?

- Do you have insecurities? What are they? Is self-doubt one of them? Is your appearance something you feel insecure about?

- Are you overconfident? Has this caused issues for you? List them.

- Do you find it difficult to compromise? Has this caused problems in your life?

- Are you competitive? Do you want to win, always?

- Are you self-motivated or do you need others to motivate you?

- Are you empathetic? Do you often reach out to others to help them with their own challenges? How does this make you feel?

- Do you feel entitled to have what others have? Why?

Reflect on Your Support System

- Do you have close friends? Do you have a strong support system of family and friends?

- Do you trust others? Is it important to you to have a trusted team of people around that you can turn to in time of need?

Reflect on Your Current Challenges

- What crisis or major challenge are you dealing with right now? Are there a lot of challenges? Can you list them and determine which is the most pressing? What are some things you can do today to address the most pressing challenge? What are some things you should do over the coming weeks to address it?

- Do you blame others for the challenges in your life? Do you feel they were caused by someone else or are someone else's fault? Remember, we make our own choices.

Reflect on Your Aspirations

- If you had one wish right now, what would it be?

- Where do you want to be in a year? Three years? Five years? Can you create a plan or describe a vision?

- Are you comfortable taking risks?

- What do you feel brings out the best version of yourself? How can you bring that best version to the world more often? What changes do you have to make?

When we take the time to do deep-dive reflection and build our playbook for moving our life path in a new direction, it gives us the chance to create the mindset we wish to live by. All of these activities require that we open ourselves up to making life changes and adapting to our new normal. Just as life throws us curveballs that force change, the build phase within my framework requires a commitment and willingness to look at our lives and make proactive changes so that we can cope with challenges better, learn from our adversities, and ultimately find greater purpose, allowing us to thrive.

CHAPTER 8

Phase 2: Build

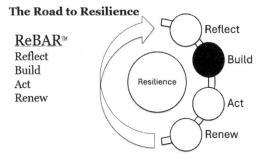

The Road to Resilience

ReBAR™
Reflect
Build
Act
Renew

Reflect

Build

Resilience

Act

Renew

There is no perfectly defined set of ingredients or tools that will help you address adversity. But if you are willing to incorporate reflection into your way of life and combine that with a willingness to make changes in your life approach based on your reflections, you are starting to move your life in a forward direction. You are entering the build phase. You are developing a growth mindset.

Success in this phase requires a mindset that allows you to see challenges as development opportunities. The key is to become comfortable with making changes on your own terms. Examples of these changes might be deciding to go to therapy, journaling every evening, or committing to reading a new book every week. Once you obtain that level of comfort by making changes to your daily routine, coping with changes that are imposed on you becomes easier, because a growth mindset allows you to navigate life's challenges with positivity and optimism, *not* fear and negativity.

Similar to the reflection phase, the build phase requires discipline. Not everyone is a fan of it, but for ReBAR to work best, discipline is essential. Discipline means a commitment to trying new approaches to deal with your challenges and sticking with them for several weeks before reflecting again to determine if you should retain or abandon those methods. Change doesn't happen overnight. Habits don't get formed overnight. The build phase is about adapting to change and approaching life with a resilience mindset. Positivity builds self-confidence because we believe we can adapt. Negativity just creates more self-doubt.

You must be willing to take some risks and step out of your comfort zone if life isn't working the way you want it to. While some types of change are imposed on us and beyond our control, we must adapt to new circumstances by focusing on those aspects that are within our control. In your personal life, when you adapt and make incremental changes in your daily routine, over time those adjustments can become life-changing. Incremental improvements may not seem to make a big impact at the moment they are made, but they can and often do become high-impact over time.

Allow yourself to absorb your reflections. Take your time to digest and process your observations. Is there something that can help you improve your way of life? Try it out if it seems promising. Building a growth mindset should not be stressful or painful.

It should be nurturing and revitalizing. Believe it or not, this practice makes life exciting. You begin to appreciate what you've learned and look forward to new opportunities that might be right around the corner—you might discover one tomorrow. Appreciate what you have today, but look forward to tomorrow and all its possibilities. That's having a positive outlook, which plays a big part in building and preparing for the act phase.

LAYING THE FOUNDATION OF THE BUILD PHASE

There are a number of elements in the build phase that are foundational to becoming comfortable with making changes in life and having the confidence that you will land in a healthier place:

- a well-structured support system
- trust and teamwork
- a positive outlook
- faith, hope, and gratitude
- life balance

A Well-Structured Support System

I had the gift of being part of a wonderful family, and I had a group of friends who were there to support and encourage me whenever I struggled. They were caring, nurturing, and committed to me. They surrounded me with positive energy.

When I was recovering in the hospital, my friend Tom showed up almost every day with a huge smile on his face and a giant milkshake to boost my spirits. My friend Tyler would sometimes pick me up from work and drive me to radiation therapy, just to make some of my days a little easier. He would wait as long as needed for me to get my therapy and be there to drive me back home to the East Bay when I was done. My mother and father were there for me every day, offering me anything and everything I might need, from taking me out to my favorite restaurants to medication pickup and lifts to and from the postoperative doctor visits that never seemed to end. My brother Rob (he now goes by the name Trebor) was there to offer moral support every day. My other brothers, Brian and Steve, visited me in the hospital every night after their long workdays were over.

In building a support system it's important to recognize those people who don't lift you up, but instead drag you down or introduce negativity into your life. Surround yourself with supportive, positive people, and distance yourself from the negative ones. Negative self-talk isn't just of our own creation. We hear negativity that directly impacts our self-confidence. Don't let negative influences make you question what makes you shine.

Remember what I wrote earlier: In times of crisis, you owe it to yourself to take care of No. 1 and surround yourself only with positive energy. The right energy is the key ingredient to your health and wellness. There is no place for negativity and doubt.

Trust and Teamwork

Some of us are skeptical of others' motives. We don't trust people until they prove they can be trusted. For me, it's the opposite. I tend to trust people until I get burned by them (should that ever happen). Regardless of your approach, finding a team of people you trust is essential to happiness and success.

In dealing with my adversity, trust came easy for me. I believed my family and friends always had my best interests at heart. I relied on them to help me make decisions about my options for surgery, treatment, and the physicians to perform surgery on me. I relied on them to help me get through dark and frightening days when I started to question whether I would survive.

I trusted my medical team when they told me they would cure me of my cancer and get me reconstructed back to the "old

Terry." Regardless of whatever the outcome was, the fact that I trusted them enabled me to keep hope throughout the process.

Hope is part of what enabled me to maintain an upbeat attitude, and hope is what allowed me to take my journey one day at a time and believe I would come out of my ordeal a better person. I was a firm believer in always remaining hopeful, and am to this day, but we all need people to keep hope real when we're on the battlefield.

Trust will help you in both your personal and professional lives. I know for a fact that I became a far more effective sales and marketing leader when I learned to trust the people who worked for me. My employees were happier and the results (the marketing research, messaging and positioning, marketing strategy, public relations plan, demand generation framework, analytics framework, sales enablement capability, etc.) were far superior. And guess what? I had a lot less stress because I trusted my people. The more trust I imparted, the better they performed. They knew I trusted their capabilities, and because they had ownership, they performed at a higher level. By trusting my team, I was helping them build their own confidence. That's a win-win!

If you want to accomplish something remarkable in business or overcome something significant in your personal life, you need a team of people you can trust. Without trust, you won't be happy with the results—guaranteed.

Try to be open and let other people into your lives, because we cannot do this thing called life alone. Your trusted circle will be your advocates, helping you regain whatever confidence you may have lost and restore your self-assurance.

A Positive Outlook

Some people believe we are pre-wired to either think positively or default on the side of negativity. I don't believe that. Positive thinking is a mindset we can train ourselves to follow. It's okay to be a realist, to think positively but prepare for the worst. That gives us a cushion for disappointment.

For me, it was always easier to focus on the positive outcome and not spend my time concerned about the risks associated with my illness, or the research and insights that would have suggested my odds of beating my disease were less than stellar.

If you act on the principles from the last two sections—surrounding yourself with positive people, and prioritizing trust and teamwork—you should feel confident that you are wiring your life for success. These elements build on themselves.

Positive thinkers are also a lot more effective in business. Do you know any executive directors or CEOs who are negative thinkers? I don't. Every business leader I know is a positive thinker. They believe in their vision and believe their business or nonprofit organization will be successful. I am certain they have their quiet moments of reflection when they have doubts, but a business leader won't last long in his or her position with a negative attitude.

Surveys of CEOs have found that regardless of whether a CEO has negative views on hiring, sales growth, or profitability, they tend to focus on areas of success rather than weakness. How can a CEO be a strong leader without having a positive outlook? How can they rally the troops to perform if there isn't, at minimum, a bullish long-term view of where the business is going?

There is such a thing as a self-fulfilling prophecy, and there are many examples of it in the real world. If a CEO forecasts negative results on an earnings call or projects softness in their upcoming business prospects, which is common, that can impact consumer sentiment and behavior. Will customers continue to buy? Should they reconsider their own buying behavior? Being optimistic doesn't mean that CEOs and business leaders don't have contingency plans and disaster plans. They do. But visionary leaders are optimists and exude positivity most of the time. I don't know about you, but I'd never work for a company with leaders who have negative prospects about the business.

Would Steve Jobs have built some of the most innovative products of all time if he didn't believe in his own ideas and in thinking differently? He believed in himself and that he and his team could deliver products the world wanted. He didn't need market research to provide the answers.

My Take on Positive Thinking

When you are confronted with adversity, you must think differently than you did before. Change is coming your way. You must find a way to believe in yourself and your ability to overcome whatever is thrown at you. You must take control and believe in a positive outcome. It makes life a whole lot easier.

But what really is positive thinking? We associate it with optimism. But it helps to unpack exactly what it is.

Positive thinking is about aiming for favorable outcomes and being able to knock down barriers along the way. Obstacles are part of life, so having a life approach that is rooted in optimism and positivity is essential to successful outcomes. And optimism reinforces your belief in self. What better way is there to continually boost your own self-confidence?

It's essential that you don't lose your enthusiasm when you are faced with new challenges. It's easy to fall into negative self-talk, but if you are aware of the pitfalls, it's also easy to remember there is always a more positive approach that can help maintain your enthusiastic spirit. That enthusiasm boosts your energy level, and having more energy is associated with improved levels of mental and physical health. How often do you get tired when you are motivated and enthused about the task at hand? Rarely or never.

As we covered earlier, you must accept hardships that come your way, but focus on positivity in your approach to addressing them.

Don't be discouraged when things aren't going your way. Pick yourself up and try again. Use your inner resources (we all have them) and ask for help if you need to. Just because you ask others for help doesn't mean you aren't confident in yourself. It just means that you trust that others can help you as well. The most confident people I know in business are very adept at using their resources to create the best outcomes and surrounding themselves with smart people (including people smarter than they are).

Most successful business leaders experienced failure at some point prior to their successes. Learn to accept failure, acknowledge it, and apply whatever learnings you acquired from it. Failure will usually benefit you in the long term. As long as you reflect on and learn from it, you can move forward. Don't dwell on failure. Use it as a springboard for improvement. (Positivity gives you motivation and strength to accomplish your goals and objectives, so remember how essential this is when you enter the act and renew phases of ReBAR.)

And when it comes to our well-being, there are a number of studies about the power of positive thinking and the impact it can have on your health. According to Johns Hopkins Medicine, "People with a family history of heart disease who also had a positive outlook were one-third less likely to have a heart attack or other cardiovascular event within five to 25 years than those with a more negative outlook . . . The finding held even in people with family history who had the most risk factors for coronary artery disease, and positive people from the general population were 13 percent less likely than their negative counterparts to have a heart attack or other coronary event."[12]

---

12   "The Power of Positive Thinking," John Hopkins Medicine, https://tinyurl.com/au8xxjw3.

Make positive thinking a part of your life.

Negative self-talk to avoid	The positive outlook alternative
I won't be able to do this.	I'll try a new approach.
I cannot improve.	I'll try again and work a little harder.
This is too difficult.	I'll approach this from a different vantage point.
I don't have all the tools I need to complete this task.	I can find a way to get it done. I'll pull in other resources if I need to.
I don't have the time.	I might be short on time, but I can re-address my priorities.
It will never work.	I will at least try to do this.
This is a huge change. I'm not sure I'm up to the task.	I won't know until I try it.

And remember what we covered earlier:

- You choose your attitude.
- You choose to fight.
- You choose to win.
- We each have the power to make our own choices.

Faith, Hope, and Gratitude

Having been raised by parents who had strong faith and believed in a higher power allowed me to build a foundation of faith throughout my childhood, and into adulthood, that gave me the courage and strength to keep hope and to soldier on. Whenever I struggle, I ask for help by praying for strength. I visualize having that strength. Whenever I strive to achieve goals that I know may be a stretch for me, I pray for extra strength and the will to achieve them.

In 1988, during my recovery and initial attempts at reconstruction, I had an experience that reinforced my belief in this higher being. My Aunt Ange, someone I always felt a special bond with, died at the ripe old age of eighty-eight. She was a wonderful woman in every way, partly demonstrated by the fact that she raised my father, Donald, from a young age after his mother passed away post-childbirth, and his father (Ange's brother) died when my father was only eleven years old. Never married or having children of her own, Ange was a hard worker who bought her own home in San Francisco and became a wonderful "grand-mother" to my three older brothers and me.

Shortly after Aunt Ange passed away, I had a dream that I still think about regularly. In the dream, my three brothers and I were gathered by her bedside, all present to say our goodbyes as she passed. (She passed alone, in reality.) She opened her eyes, rose from her bed, grabbed my hand, looked me in the eye, and said, "Life is full of struggles, but in the end it will all be worth it."

I reflect on that dream to this day. It was not scary in any way. It reinforced my belief in the afterlife and the strong connection I always felt to Aunt Ange. It was so powerful that it's one of only a few dreams I can remember clearly to this day. I felt she chose to say those words to me in the dream because she knew I was struggling and needed strength to carry on more than anyone else at that particular time.

Since that day, I have always referred to Aunt Ange as my guardian angel. I pray to her directly sometimes because I still feel she has a connection to the Holy Spirit that no one else I know has.

Every year in December, our family watches *It's a Wonderful Life*, starring James Stewart and Donna Reed. We always look forward to the ending when Stewart's character, George Bailey, holds his daughter in front of the Christmas tree, a happy and fulfilled man once again.

Shortly before that moment, George had gone back to the bridge he was going to jump from because of his hopelessness and begged Clarence (his guardian angel) for his life back. Clarence granted his wish, and George rushed home to await his arrest in regard to some missing money. When he arrived, he saw that Mary and Uncle Billy had rallied all the townspeople to collectively donate more than enough to replace the money.

His brother Harry arrives shortly thereafter and toasts George as "the richest man in town."

George then finds a copy of *The Adventures of Tom Sawyer* hidden in the donations from the townspeople—a gift from Clarence. George opens it, and inscribed inside are the words, "Remember, no man is a failure who has friends. Thanks for the wings!"

A moment later, a bell on the Christmas tree rings. George's daughter Zuzu looks up at her father with a smile, saying, "Every time a bell rings, an angel gets his wings." George smiles and whispers, "That's right. That's right." He then looks heavenward and says, "Attaboy, Clarence."

Whenever I watch that scene, I look heavenward and say to myself (and sometimes my wife), "Attagirl, Ange."

Being grateful has always been important to me. I thank God for the gifts he has given me every day. And believe me, I am grateful for the gift of cancer. I am a more caring and empathetic person for the experience. I learned at a very young age about the fragility of life. I am now able to put things into perspective and am less prone to sweat the small stuff. Part of my life ministry became helping others to deal with their own adversities, and that remains to this day. That's the true gift and why I remain grateful every day.

Even though people experience completely different types of adversities and trauma, many believe their personal challenge is what ultimately led them to success in their careers. In *David and Goliath*, Malcolm Gladwell writes about several successful businesspeople who, because of their dyslexia and personal difficulties, were forced to create coping mechanisms and unique learning approaches to develop valuable skills that those without learning disabilities don't think to consider in their own development. Their disadvantages may have become their advantages. Examples of those with dyslexia include the following: Gary Cohn, who became the president and chief operating officer of Goldman Sachs and the director of the National Economic Council; David Boies, one of the world's most famous trial lawyers; finance executive Charles Schwab; Virgin Group co-founder Richard Branson; and a host of others. Would they wish dyslexia on anyone else? No. Are they grateful for it in their own lives? Yes. It made them who they are. As Gary Cohn said in *David and Goliath*, "I wouldn't be where I am today without my dyslexia."[13]

Gary Payton II ("GPII"), an NBA basketball player and son of Gary Payton, a nine-time NBA all-star, got to the bottom of his own dyslexia challenge. With the support of his mother, he became an advocate for others with dyslexia by founding his own nonprofit, the GPII Foundation. When they learned of GPII's dyslexia, his mother reached out to actor Henry Winkler, also known as the Fonz from *Happy Days*, who helped them understand his learning disability and how to cope with it. GPII was able to change the trajectory of his life and graduated from Oregon State University with a degree in human development and family science.[14] Outside of his demanding NBA career, GPII is on a mission to support "early screening, detection, and certified assessment for youth and young adults with languages-based learning challenges."[15] Adversity can not only change us, but help to change the lives of so many others.

My faith has also served as a blueprint for helping others. As I mentioned earlier, the poem "Footprints" represents my faith in so many ways and has served as my compass for giving back whenever

13 Malcolm Gladwell, *David and Goliath: Underdogs, Misfits, and the Art of Battling Giants* (New York: Back Bay Books / Little, Brown and Company, 2013), 97–124.

14 Monte Poole, "GP2 Continues to Pay It Forward After Life-Changing Diagnosis," NBC Sports Bay Area, November 16, 2023, https://www.nbcsportsbayarea.com/nba/golden-state-warriors/gary-payton-ii-dyslexia/1681944.

15 GPII Foundation, https://gpiifoundation.org/.

possible. Helping others when they need to be lifted up, or just being present when others need support, has become a way of life for me.

I am fortunate that people find me on the internet and reach out to me when they are confronted with sarcoma cancers or are threatened with facial differences resulting from their cancers. Many want to talk to someone who has been through what they are facing, some are seeking physician recommendations, and others are just at a loss on how to move forward. Some seem to be losing hope.

I offer words of encouragement but am careful to communicate that I can only offer the perspective of a patient. I am always honest and share the risks that reconstruction may present (using examples from my own experience of what can go wrong) but try to focus on positivity, whatever the prognosis is that lies ahead of them. I always, always encourage them to keep hope and be sure they like and trust the doctors providing their care. I close all conversations by telling them I will keep them in my prayers and think positive thoughts for them.

If all of us could row in the same direction in life, with the aim of helping our fellow men and women in times of need, we'd certainly find more peace, more happiness, and fewer disappointments and failures. I am a firm believer in collective consciousness and the power of positive energy. Together we are so much stronger. Apart, we are fractured.

Life Balance

All of us struggle with finding the time to balance our priorities. Daily pressures can make it difficult to do the things we know we should do—eat right, get enough sleep, get enough exercise. As we covered earlier with finding time for daily reflection, we owe it to ourselves to prioritize our lives with a long-term view in mind. Our mental, physical, emotional, and spiritual health can erode day by day if we don't focus on taking care of ourselves and loving ourselves first.

But how can we achieve this?

You must be organized to find a way to instill new daily routines that can become habits. Set a time every day to exercise and carve the time out on your calendar. Find time to go to the grocery store so that you have healthy food in the house to enjoy. Aim to get to bed at the same time every night, within reason, of course. Having some flexibility is critical to happiness too, and so is allowing yourself rewards from time to time that will make your routines worthwhile.

It might sound boring, but I guarantee that if you prioritize and build muscle memory into your daily life, you will find greater happiness. And you will have less stress in your life, not more. At first, it might sound onerous. Finding time to exercise and cook healthy foods every day can seem taxing, but in time, once the habits are formed, you will not only feel better physically but emotionally and mentally as well. And guess what? You'll notice you have greater confidence.

I discovered that having life balance and exercising not only improved my mood throughout the day, but the positive impact on my self-confidence was so clear to me that it kept me continually motivated to carve out that special time for myself. As I felt better about the way I looked, I began to carry myself with more confidence, and my stress level seemed reduced.

The reality is that many of us are stressed out, and this can often lead to health challenges. Part of life balance is having outlets. Finding an outlet can be the best form of stress release. Think of outlets as things you have always wanted to try or learn. They could be hobbies you just haven't had the time to explore.

Because many of us are getting information from our mobile devices seemingly 24/7, we never escape from the pressures of work or the stressors of newsfeeds. We jump from meetings to work tasks to family tasks but rarely find time to step back and release our tensions by doing something we love that makes us feel energized—like going for a walk or bike ride, working out, surfing, or playing music.

For our mental health, I am a firm believer in having outlets, activities we love 100 percent or those we want to try for the first time. A wonderful byproduct of outlets is that oftentimes it's when we are in the midst of enjoying them that we come up with our best ideas, new innovative approaches to solving a business problem, or new tactics that might help us confront challenges or relationships we're struggling with.

When you open your mind to an outlet that requires your full attention and free yourself from multitasking, you not only feel refreshed, but you remove mental clutter so that you have a clear mind to think more creatively. The best managers encourage employees to take time for themselves, not guilt them into working 24/7. Finding those managers isn't easy, but finding employment with businesses that embrace that type of culture can prove rewarding and improve your chances for success. Being fully transparent with your manager that you joined an ice hockey team, that you took up piano, that you took up sewing—whatever it is—also relieves stress because you and your manager know what's going on in your life outside of work. Secrets don't help. They always cause more stress.

Some of my outlets have been part of my routine for as long as I can remember, while others I bring into my life when I am inspired to try to improve myself in other ways. What's key is that these outlets should not create additional stress in your life. They should be things you look forward to but are also attainable within the life schedule you have. Don't set overly ambitious goals, because if you fail, you'll be less inclined to set new goals and develop new outlets, and that can negatively impact your self-confidence.

I have always found that what works best for my mental, physical, emotional, and spiritual well-being is having an exercise routine that I try to perform every morning. If I miss two days a week, I don't beat myself up. But even when I travel, I perform bodyweight workouts in my hotel room, or I use the hotel gym. By mixing cardiovascular exercise with weightlifting, I find my whole body feels revitalized just as I start my day. I also find I work out the kinks and pains I sometimes wake up with. I am less irritable during the day and am more self-confident.

Over the years, I found I was becoming stressed out by 6 p.m. because I'd been in meetings and working nonstop for eleven hours straight. I didn't want to just leave my office, go home, and head to the kitchen to help my wife prepare dinner. I needed something for me.

After watching and appreciating skilled guitarists all my life, I decided I wanted to learn how to play the acoustic guitar. I started to take lessons one evening a week. On other evenings I would grab my guitar and practice my lessons and new songs in my songbook. I aimed to practice for thirty minutes, but if I could find only twenty minutes, I didn't beat myself up.

I was so excited to learn to play. Playing guitar was the perfect release, even though I wasn't very good. I don't have an ear for music. I couldn't listen to a song and hear the G chord, the C chord, or differentiate a D minor from a D major. My teacher had to write the music in my songbook. That meant I had to concentrate on the sequence of chord changes and strum patterns 100 percent of the time I played. I had not built muscle memory yet, and that was the best part. I forgot about my other deadlines for that thirty-minute practice period every night. The only way for me to learn was to concentrate and rehearse continuously, with no disruptions.

When that routine started to become stressful after four years of having to fit in the time every single night, I decided it was okay to drop it from my daily routine and play when I felt like it. Now, in the spring, summer, and fall, I try to get out for an hour-long mountain bike ride or play a few holes of golf because I prefer being outdoors to indoors whenever possible. When I am mountain biking on challenging trails, I am focused and cannot think about my other duties. I need to concentrate—or

I'll crash! (In fact, I have lost focus while riding and done that!) Playing golf requires that I focus on my next shot, or God knows where the ball will fly (or not fly!). That's the power of outlets. They're enjoyable, but they require your full attention. Enjoy life. If you do, mundane tasks will be much easier to manage because you can bookend them with outlets you enjoy.

If you are looking for hard facts on why life balance is important, the numbers are mind-boggling. In a mental health survey conducted by Ipsos in October 2022,[16] the following details of adults' rising stress levels emerged:

- About three in five adults both in the U.S. (56%) and around the world (62%) said that stress affected their daily lives at least once in the past year. One-third (35% in the U.S. and 34% globally) said stress affected their daily lives several times.
- Almost as many said they felt stressed to the point where they "could not cope or deal with things" at least once (52% in the U.S. and 60% globally), including three in ten (29% and 31%, respectively) several times.
- Among respondents who were employed, four in ten (36% in the U.S. and 39% globally) reported having felt so stressed that they could not go to work for a period of time at least once in the last year.
- About half of adults in the U.S. (46%) and globally (52%) said they have felt sad or hopeless almost every day for a couple of weeks or more at least once in the past year.

We need life balance. We need stress release. We need outlets to reduce our stress.

---

16 "Majority of Adults Report Experiencing High Levels of Stress in Past Year," Ipsos, October 5, 2022, https://www.ipsos.com/en-us/news-polls/world-mental-health-day -monitor-2022.

HOW I TOOK RISKS TO ADAPT

By adapting my approach to life, I was able to motivate myself and begin to take actions that would become truly transformational turning points I never expected or anticipated until they became part of my routine. As I began to set goals, I realized I could become unstoppable. I started to feel like I truly could triumph over my trauma.

I reflected on my life. I decided to write a memoir about my experience overcoming my cancer and facial difference. Writing was therapeutic, and getting the book published was an accomplishment. I was proud of the journey I was on. I began to entertain the idea of doing speaking engagements to share my story.

Because I was gaining more confidence every day, I began to take more risks. In 2001, instead of chasing another position in a high-tech firm, I took a chance on myself. Previously, I was senior VP of marketing for a software services company, and we were fortunate with market timing to go public via an IPO in February 1999. I was grateful for the monetary freedom that provided, so I decided it was time for a change. I decided to go into consulting.

I started working with start-ups, serving as interim VP of marketing in the high-tech sector. I realized I needed multiple assignments to fill my schedule and maximize my income. I figured I would typically need two or three consulting engagements at any one time to get there. I realized that my value was increasing and my knowledge base was expanding as I began consulting. The opportunities kept coming. I needed to learn about each business sector my clients were operating in so that I could provide value and help them best position themselves for success. I had to be a quick study and to prioritize my time more than ever before.

My business expanded, and my income grew. I shifted my focus from start-ups to larger, more mature technology companies, because I knew that business development within those organizations would be easier than finding another new start-up to consult for whenever I finished an assignment as interim VP of marketing. I began working with Intel and then Cisco Systems, both large high-tech companies with multiple business units within them. My exposure to these units made identifying new opportunities easier and easier.

My confidence grew. I was building a trusted brand for myself. And I was in control. Yes, I had to report to each client and be available to them, but I ultimately controlled my schedule. I began to add more speaking engagements into my schedule to share my personal story. I became passionate about inspiring students, healthcare professionals, and corporate employees to take control of their own lives, learn to build trusting teams, and overcome challenges.

I was reflecting. I was adapting. And I was motivated and passionate about what I was doing. I was taking action. I was willing to take a risk on myself because I believed in myself more than ever before.

Challenges as Growth Opportunities

Let's go back to the early nineties again. This is the essential background behind what eventually led me to believe I could take more risks.

I had a big challenge I knew I needed to address, but I was terrified by the prospect of even trying to deal with it. Over a period of a few years, I had spiraled downward after learning in 1991 that my facial difference would be permanent. Yes, Dina, the woman who accompanied me to the wine country and told me I needed to work on my issues, helped to set me on a new course, but it would take a lot of work. I lacked the confidence I once had and shied away from things that had once seemed so natural to me.

I reflected on my life. As mentioned earlier, I decided to write a memoir about my experience overcoming my cancer. My work life was very time-consuming, but I finally got the book published. I pushed myself to do speaking engagements to promote it. But I still wasn't comfortable having to present in front of groups of people during that time. It filled me with anxiety. Because of my facial difference, I had come to expect that people wouldn't take me seriously. I had become afraid of being judged and ridiculed, and having to face any large group of people amplified that fear. Quite honestly, I had become incredibly insecure. But I somehow kept up a strong front so that people at work, and those on my team, didn't see it like I did. I worked hard and overprepared, so I always appeared buttoned-up in meetings.

Initially, I was given opportunities to present my story at bookstores, to associations, and to nonprofits in the cancer support and research arena. Then I began to get approached by healthcare organizations and hospitals as I received media attention in publications like *NurseWeek*, *Guideposts*, *Psychology Today*, the *San Francisco Examiner*, the *San Francisco Chronicle*, the *Oakland Tribune*, and others. Soon, corporations, professional associations, and schools began to reach out.

At that point, no one asked me for a demo reel or a video of my past speaking engagements. They just wanted to hear my story. If I wanted to get my message out to the world, I had to get comfortable presenting regularly, and I soon discovered people were interested in what I had to say and were not prejudging me based on a past performance I'd given.

I prepared and rehearsed my material. I figured if I was well prepared for whatever audience I'd be presenting to, I'd start to become more and more confident in how I delivered my messages and engaged the audience. I wasn't trying to memorize my material, but I had been working in a professional environment long enough to know that I needed to present a clear and engaging story or no one would listen.

I learned that preparation and practice made me more comfortable and confident. I approached each presentation with the same level of preparation, never taking for granted that just because my last presentation went well meant the next one would too.

I heard a story about Johnny Carson around this time that was so relatable. An interviewer was talking to him about his late-night show and complimenting him on his ability to be so incredibly engaging and comfortable with his audience. She asked if he ever got nervous. His answer surprised me.

He said he got nervous and had butterflies before every single show. He added that the day he wasn't nervous before a show was the day he would quit. Nerves drove him to be sure he was well versed and well prepared before walking out on stage. Hearing this story inspired me and helped me realize that being successful isn't about having gifts others may have been blessed with. Anyone can be successful with hard work, focus, dedication, and preparation.

Focusing on one presentation at a time helped me achieve my goal. My focus was singular and short-term—to nail the next presentation. The beauty about focus is that every time you face one of your challenges or achieve one of your goals, it gives you that much more confidence to face the next one, so you begin to recognize there is nothing you cannot achieve if you stay focused and knock down one goal at a time. (I have more to say about focus in chapter 9.) But remember: one goal at a time. Don't stretch yourself too thin and set multiple goals, or you will get overwhelmed.

My confidence and self-esteem continued to grow. I had faced a major challenge and overcome it in a way I never expected I could. Don't ever underestimate yourself!

BUILD YOUR RESILIENCE MINDSET

Putting the Build Phase into Practice

The build phase is all about preparation. It is how we prepare mentally, emotionally, physically, and spiritually to face and defeat adversity. While this may sound like a huge undertaking, small steps add up to big success. Keep this perspective in mind.

Reflect on Your Current Challenges

- Are you ready to set a new goal and begin to put it into practice? Are there some short-term steps you can take? Are there longer-term steps you can visualize?

- Is there something you were inspired by over the past week that you're ready to act on?

- Is there something you are doing that warrants a different approach to produce a different outcome?

Reflect on Your Aspirations

- From your deep-dive reflection, are there some big changes you are ready to commit to? Write them down and insert a start date.

- Have you determined what your one-year plan is yet? What about your three-year and five-year plans? Are you ready to start building these plans by documenting the actions you need to take this week, next week, next month?

Reflect on Ways to Find Strength

- What is your confidence level like? Now that you are trying new approaches to making progress in your life, are you feeling more confident that you can adapt? Are you thinking about possibilities instead of limitations? Remember, a growth mindset instills positivity and helps reinforce that you can learn from every challenge.

- Are you more comfortable with the idea that you can meet change with courage? Remember, courage counteracts any fear or uncertainty that we may have and helps us build our confidence. Take a small risk and see how it goes. There is no such thing as failure, only learning.

- Are you surrounded by positive people and a strong support system? What are the ways you gain strength from your support team? Do you show your gratitude?

- Do you naturally have a positive attitude, or do you find yourself grappling with negative self-talk? Can you think about some recent examples when you struggled to find the silver lining in your misfortune and think about the alternative, positive approach to take instead?

- Is faith something that gives you strength? Do people you trust give you hope?

- Can you find gratitude in your misfortune and use it as the springboard for change? Is there something about your misfortune that has made you take a different path toward your accomplishments? Recognize that and remember it. You may find it a helpful tool in the future.

- Are you able to take time for yourself? Do you have life balance? If not, what can you do to bring more balance into your life?

In sum, the ability to adapt is the offspring of daily reflection. Naturally, you don't expect everything that you reflect on to become life-changing, but when you practice reflection you'll find that over time it becomes easier to identify new opportunities to address your challenges. As you try these out, you may decide to assimilate them into your daily routines. If a new idea doesn't work out the way you thought, that's okay. The key is to take those few minutes every day to reflect and think about the possibilities, not the limitations, and to improve on how you are managing your life for success, happiness, and purpose.

The act phase is the next one in the framework, and that is where the rubber meets the road. The work you have done in the reflect and build phases will be a platform for taking the actions needed for a more fulfilling life.

CHAPTER 9

Phase 3: Act

The Road to Resilience

ReBAR™
Reflect
Build
Act
Renew

Reflect

Build

Resilience

Act

Renew

The act phase is when you begin to take control, face challenges head-on, set higher and harder goals, and consider adding therapy, visualization, meditation, and yoga to your routine so that your emotional and physical health continue to improve. For me, finding the motivation and ability to execute my action plan wasn't difficult. Did it take work? Yes. Was it attainable? Yes.

How did I develop the plan? I had to focus on one thing at a time. Put one action into motion before adding the next one to your plate. Too much too soon can result in frustration and failure, and that can impact your self-confidence in a negative way. That's why, if you continue to focus on taking single steps and not giant leaps, your confidence will grow. You'll see the results.

For me, the key elements of my plan were and continue to be the following:

- gaining perspective and control
- finding ways to defeat insecurity
- knowing where to put my focus
- setting meaningful goals
- employing outlets and hobbies, and striving for work-life balance
- using therapy to find my courage within
- practicing visualization/guided imagery
- practicing mindfulness and meditation
- practicing yoga

FROM VISION TO ACTION PLAN

Gaining Perspective

I have written a lot about Dina and the impact she had on me after our brief relationship. She helped me realize that the scars I had developed on the inside were much worse than the scars on the outside. I reflected on her assessment for some time and realized she was right. What turned people away was not my physical appearance, but my insecurity and need for reassurance.

As I reflected on Dina's poignant words, everything started to come into a clearer perspective, and I began to realize I didn't need to fixate on my next reconstructive procedure any longer. I had to focus on rebuilding what was inside.

Clearly, I could not control the outcomes of any of my surgical procedures. I was taking two steps back for every step forward due to the complexity of my case and its impact on my eye, nose, cheek, and upper lip. My surgeons seemed surprised that my appearance wasn't improving to the degree they'd hoped. Up until that point, I was still expecting and believing that reconstruction would fix my physical appearance and deformity, and that the results of those surgeries would solve whatever insecurities I had developed. I never considered what was happening inside of me during that time and the damage that was being done to my psyche.

A light bulb came on when I finally realized that surgery was never going to fix my insecurities. Even if the surgery appeared successful, I knew I was always going to be my own worst critic. I would notice the imperfections more than anyone else. I probably would never really be satisfied with the results. I had to find a way to rebuild myself from the inside out and find a way to love myself again, for who I was and not for what I looked like.

Upon reflection, I realized group and individual therapy was something I had to try. Maybe I could begin to accept who I was and find contentment. If I could accept who I was, become grateful my life was spared, and find a way to stop constantly seeking reassurance, I could begin to address the insecurity that was swallowing my whole being.

Participating in group therapy proved incredibly valuable for me. It was cathartic to share and talk with members of my support group at the Cancer Support Community about things I couldn't talk about to my family and friends. I felt liberated that I could speak honestly and openly about my insecurities. I listened to others who shared their own fears and insecurities with the group—they feared death and worried about their families and the burden their illnesses would have on those who depended upon them.

I found it was therapeutic to offer my own words of wisdom to them—things they hadn't considered that would help them find peace and purpose. I encouraged them not to allow themselves to dwell on their illnesses and their fears, but to set new goals that would inspire them to rise every morning with a newfound purpose and renewed hope for the day ahead. After all, none of us knows what tomorrow will bring.

I began to realize that expressing my vulnerabilities and insecurities was the first step in beginning to address them. Others told me that what I had experienced and overcome to that point in my life was inspirational, and that I was strong and courageous.

Gaining Control

I began to realize that group therapy was enabling me to find even more courage. I was stepping outside of my comfort zone, had something unique to offer, and could contribute in a positive way in this world, just like everyone else. I could start to take control of where my life was going because my self-confidence was improving after every group session.

I was inspired to change my life and take more risks, and I felt recharged driving home from my support groups, even though it was typically 9 p.m., and I had already worked a full day. I was already beginning to feel a sense of renewal and restoration, and I was excited about the path in front of me. I reflected some more. How could I truly take control and put myself in the driver's seat of life?

I thought about my job. Although the hours were long, I felt like I was making a difference. I had become aware that the CEO empowered his people to make recommendations and improvements to the business so that we could scale up more quickly. He was encouraging innovation from everyone in the company, regardless of their experience or role. Why couldn't I be one of the change agents?

As I reflected on that, I realized I couldn't just work hard to get recognition—I had to work smart. What could I do differently? How could I improve our customer service process? I knew there was a ton of room for improvement. Later, as I moved into a new role, I began to consider how I could drive costs out of our product line management function and negotiate deeper discounts. As I dedicated myself to the business and to making a difference, I started to see rewards. I was promoted, and new opportunities became available to me. My change of focus was helping me to grow, learn, and most importantly rebuild the confidence and self-esteem that I had lost over the past few years.

I continued to focus on my work, and I found a lot of success. By the time I was thirty, I was promoted to vice president of regional marketing, and then a year later, we were acquired by a public company; instead of losing my job in a reorganization as typically happens, I was promoted to VP of national marketing. We sold the business to another public company, and the CEO, Peter Jackson, my mentor, hired me again to be the senior VP of marketing for another start-up idea he had come up with. Within four years, we took that company public. I began consulting for venture capitalists as well as for large, high-growth technology companies. Later, I went back to a venture-backed company as a vice president. I was setting my agenda. I was controlling where I wanted to go.

What I loved about what I did over those many years was working with highly competitive people who wanted to not only make a difference but make an impact on the markets we served. I was surrounded by passionate people and I trusted their intentions. This experience never seemed to be about just having a job. It was about measuring success, finding fulfillment, and being open to the next opportunity that might be right around the corner.

By practicing self-care and finding work-life balance, I had begun to restore my identity. I was proud of my accomplishments, proud of my recovery, proud of my triumph over harrowing cancer, and grateful that I had positioned myself well enough to share my successes with others who were struggling with their own adversities.

I had a newfound perspective on life. Every day was intentional. That's one of the most profound gifts that come from our adversities—gaining perspective and being able to look at the big picture, not the small stuff that doesn't really matter.

My focus and determination to rebuild myself might have been assembled from many scattered puzzle pieces, but ultimately I had found a way to cobble them together and develop a vision that not only works for me, but I hope for you as well, so that you too can feel like you are in the driver's seat of life.

Taking control of what we can control, and not focusing on what we cannot, allows us to keep focused and stay positive. Call it being selfish, but we owe it to ourselves to love ourselves first. Only then can you love others. As I shared earlier, that was a tough, tough lesson for me.

Focusing on what we can control allows us to eliminate anxiety and worry, which drain our critical energy resources. We cannot control other people's actions and reactions, only our own.

We cannot control the past—what happened, happened. We often reflect on our adversities and wonder what we did wrong— what led to our divorce, what led to our job loss, what caused us to be in an abusive relationship. That can be a beneficial exercise if the intention is to uncover and learn from past actions and reactions and figure out how we can act differently in the future. But we should not dwell on the past. Reflect, note those thoughts to yourself, and move forward. Set your course for the future.

If we focus on what we can control, like being present and expressing gratitude for all we have, it allows us to develop the mindset for success in our personal and professional lives. Taking control of your life reinforces your self-belief.

Taking control is about attitude, preparation, and the effort we put in to set our course in a direction we desire. Countless research studies prove that when patients experiencing disease feel in control, they have increased rates of survival.

As I began to take control of my own life, my perception of myself changed. Over time, instead of looking in the mirror and having moments of disappointment about the way I looked, I began to see battle scars that made me proud of who I was.

Defeating Insecurity

We all wrestle with insecurity. For me, it took something devastating to recognize that my battle scars are a gift that has given me wisdom I lacked before. Looking at myself in the mirror reminds me every day to put life into perspective. It reminds me that my scars are a testament to my strength, courage, and the limitless opportunities I have in front of me. I can stand in front of the mirror on my own two legs. I can see, I can hear, and I can move my arms, hands, and fingers. I can feel the thickness of my scars and remind myself that they represent healing, not pain.

My battle scars remind me why I am grateful for my experience. I appreciate every day of my life, and I am more forgiving and tolerant than ever before. I have more empathy than ever before. There is no one to blame. I learned from my experience, and I'm grateful that I can now help so many others by reminding them that attitude is what makes all the difference.

Attitude is about what you can do in the present. Here. Now. It's not worrying about the future, which you cannot control.

Knowing Where to Put Your Focus

Don't try to do too much or spread yourself too thin. When we know what to focus on, our odds of success improve.

In his book *Dealing with Darwin*,[17] Geoffrey Moore drills down into this concept and provides myriad examples of what

---

17 Geoffrey A. Moore, *Dealing with Darwin: How Great Companies Innovate at Every Phase of Their Evolution* (New York: Portfolio, 2005).

"core versus context" is in the real world. In the business world, core is what customers are willing to pay for, while context is what they don't necessarily care about. More simply said, a business should hire employees able to focus on the unique value proposition of the business, or "secret sauce."

A consumer-packaged goods company, for example, needs to invest in core activities such as AI-powered analytics, enhancing customer engagement, addressing new wellness trends, and focusing on digital transformation to streamline operations. At the same time, such a company will see business improvements by outsourcing context activities, such as finding its next manufacturing plant or managing its data center requirements.

For professional golfer Tiger Woods, golf has always been core to him, while advertising endorsements are context. The endorsement deals bring in an incredible amount of money for Tiger, but without his success in golf he wouldn't even have endorsements. He knows where he should focus.

Mark Nevins, a *Forbes* contributor who specializes in leadership strategy, asks his clients every January what their Big Rocks (aka priorities) are.[18] The Big Rocks concept was popularized by Stephen Covey in his book *The Seven Habits of Highly Effective People*, and it adeptly illustrates the importance of focus in achieving business and personal success.[19] The Big Rocks concept is a lesson in time management and prioritizing your most important personal and professional priorities, and is best demonstrated using rocks, gravel, and sand.

To illustrate the concept, visualize an empty jar, which represents your time, while the rocks, gravel, and sand represent priorities and tasks. Rocks represent the most important tasks, while gravel is less important, and finally, sand represents trivial

---

18   Mark Nevins, "What Are Your Big Rocks?" *Forbes*, January 21, 2020, https://www.forbes.com/sites/hillennevins/2020/01/21/what-are-your-big-rocks/?sh=5dd5ea09fae3.

19   Stephen R. Covey, *The 7 Habits of Highly Effective People: Powerful Lessons in Personal Change* (New York: Simon & Schuster, 2003).

tasks and distractions that can be very time consuming. If you put the rocks in the jar first, there will still be room for gravel and sand. But if you put the gravel and sand in first, there won't be room for the rocks. The message is that you need to focus first and foremost on the most important priorities (the rocks), and you will likely find time for the less important tasks. If you focus on context activities first, you will never achieve your most critical priorities.

Setting Meaningful Goals

Focus for me became a lot about setting goals and persevering. I set personal and professional goals with timelines. Some of them were short term (running a 10K race in under thirty-six minutes, bench-pressing three hundred pounds, getting promoted, taking on additional responsibility at work, learning new skills), while others I would set two to three years out (getting my own place to live, getting bigger promotions, building teams, expanding my skill set even more broadly).

Were these goals realistic or were they out of my comfort zone? I'd say somewhere between. There's a difference between dreaming big in life and overcoming an obstacle or adversity right in front of you. You can always dream big, but it helps to set individual goals on the path to that big dream when adversity and obstacles need to be overcome first.

You hear a lot about dreaming big in sports and in business and achieving anything you set your mind to. There's a place for that, for sure. But achieving individual goals along the way gives you the confidence you need to know you can knock down your goals. Each time you knock one down, you have more confidence to focus on the next goal. Self-doubt becomes a thing of the past. Each new goal can be more aspirational.

I found that the time-bound goals I set for myself gave me a clear purpose and prevented me from dwelling on my illness, my facial difference, and other things that would only cause me anxiety and worry. I found the mix of personal and professional goals to be therapeutic for a number of reasons:

- While I was always looking forward to what was coming next, I also relished living in the here and now.
- I was making better choices every day despite whatever negative energy I was experiencing.
- I was developing personally and professionally.
- I was achieving goals, which boosted my confidence.
- I was happier.

I was lucky that I didn't overextend by setting too many goals. When we do that, we often find our ability to accomplish anything becomes compromised. That's when frustration sets in. That's why new year's resolutions fail so often. I cringe when employers talk to their associates about setting their top ten resolutions for the new year. That's too many!

In *Be Your Future Self Now*,[20] Dr. Benjamin Hardy refers to Jim Collins's book *Good to Great*, where Jim explains the difference between highly successful companies and good companies. In my opinion, his advice applies to our personal lives as well: "If you have more than three priorities, you have none."[21]

Dr. Hardy goes on to explain the single purpose he had as a teenager, which was to go on a church mission after high school. He did not have a clear picture of what his life would look like after that mission, but he believed that was the most important thing he could do at that time for his future self. When he returned from his mission, he had improved clarity. He set his *contextual purpose* for what he believed were the most important things he

---

20   Dr. Benjamin Hardy, *Be Your Future Self Now: The Science of Intentional Transformation* (New York: Hay House, 2022).

21   Ibid., 174.

could do right now (a concept derived from the work of Viktor Frankl, a survivor of Nazi concentration camps and author of *The Doctor and the Soul* and *Man's Search for Meaning*). He set his *contextual purpose* (his three most important objectives) for the next five years, then the next five years after that. He achieved every one of those goals.[22]

Howard Schultz, the founder of Starbucks, was rejected by two hundred investors before he was able to get sufficient financing to launch his company. It took Agatha Christie five years before she found a publisher for her first book. They both had a single-minded goal, but without perseverance, they would never have achieved their incredible success.[23]

Remember, we make choices every day. Don't allow yourself to get caught up in the context of your life. Instead focus on your goals. Persevere.

~~~~~~

Although I haven't written about grit per se, my ability to overcome my adversity and rebuild my confidence is a result of my grit and perseverance. I was never the smartest, most athletic, or most confident person, but I had the drive to work hard and to learn from my failures to find success because I made reflection and goal-setting a part of my life. Motivational speaker and author Caroline Adams Miller, in her blog post "How to Get More Grit: 10 Traits That Every Authentically Gritty Person Needs," wrote that many of the traits of authentic grit are about having passion, and many of the traits can be learned.[24] People with grit tend to be more hopeful, goal-oriented, and optimistic, and that leads to resilience and the ability to bounce back.

22   Hardy, 130–136.

23   Eileen S. Lenson, *Overcoming Adversity: Conquering Life's Challenges* (Melbourne: Australian Academic Press, 2018), 147–148.

24   Caroline Adams Miller, blog post, October 10, 2017, https://www.carolinemiller.com/ authentically-gritty/.

> Perseverance and grit are about refusing to give up and remaining persistent despite whatever roadblocks enter our path. My training for an upcoming race may have gotten derailed sometimes due to another reconstructive surgical procedure, but the doctors always knew I'd be asking when I could work out again so that I could remain focused on my goal. That's relentless perseverance.

Employing Outlets and Hobbies, and Striving for Work-Life Balance

Often we find ourselves working long days, taking care of family chores, or spending all day in class and after-school activities, and then coming home to do other chores to keep our households running. Typically, before retiring to bed, we sit down to read our email, finish the presentation we have to deliver the next day, or complete a homework assignment. On weekends, we often have a list of personal things that need to get done. Somehow the list always seems to be getting longer. Before we know it, we find a level of dissatisfaction or lack of fulfillment because we feel like we're just going through the motions to keep up with our day-to-day lives.

We all need to take time for ourselves and find outlets that we can also focus on outside of the day-to-day stressors of life. We all need to find time to unwind and to decompress.

For me, that's getting exercise every morning. As previously mentioned, I mix cardiovascular exercise with weights, and afterward I feel refreshed and excited about my day ahead. On days I don't find the time for my workout, I tend to be crankier, sometimes shorter with people, and less excited about my day. The reason I get cranky is because when I skip my exercise, I plunge right into my workday without taking any time for myself. I allow it to happen. I need to reflect and do my best to not let that happen whenever possible.

Some people start their day with meditation. Others find that taking a quiet walk in the morning does the trick. Whatever works for you is the answer.

Listen to yourself and listen to your body. We know when we need to step away and focus 100 percent on something that brings us joy or brings us release.

As I wrote about earlier in the book, I took on a new outlet when I began to feel stressed after work. Learning to play the acoustic guitar was a much-needed outlet for me, because I had to focus entirely on the techniques I was learning for the song to come out right (or almost right, in my case). If I thought about my work or the chores I needed to complete that evening, my guitar practice would at best be non-productive, and at worst turn into an utter failure.

One of the most rewarding and productive parts about employing outlets is that sometimes my best ideas come to me when I am doing exactly what I want to do in my own quiet time. We have all heard people talk about this concept. My doctor used to tell me he got his best ideas in the shower. Employees come up with innovative ideas when they are away from their desks and not in meetings. They come up with new ideas when their minds are open and not cluttered with daily stressors. Often our best ideas come to us while we're on vacation. Give it a shot. You'll be glad you did.

Are you stressed out? Do you feel like you are banging your head against the wall and not making the progress that you need to? Do you feel like you are in a funk?

Think about what makes you happy. Is it being outdoors? Is it writing? Is it painting? Is it playing music? Is it playing games with your children?

In your notebook or journal, write down some things that bring you joy. Then write down which of them you can fit into your daily routine. If you could allocate thirty to sixty minutes per day to doing something that lifts you up and excites you, what would it be?

After you have written these ideas down, look over your list. What seems the most promising and viable? Which activity do you think you would find the most success with in your daily routine?

It's okay to try something and find it doesn't work. Try something else if it isn't giving you the joy and outlet you need. If it just adds more stress to your life, it's probably a poor choice. But it takes about two weeks to create a routine, so try whatever it is for two weeks before deciding to move on to something else. Or maybe you like the outlet, but it's taking too much time. Scale back the time commitment to twenty minutes from thirty.

Using Therapy to Find Courage Within

I have discussed therapy in various sections of the book, but I wanted to call it out in the act phase separately because therapy and the courage it gave me were so instrumental in my path forward. As I mentioned before, I began to share my vulnerabilities and talk with other cancer patients about issues and concerns that I couldn't talk about to my own family. It was a cathartic experience, and by expressing my vulnerabilities, I felt like I had newfound courage to take on the world.

Opening myself up was liberating. By opening up to others, I took myself out of my comfort zone and felt more courageous. After all, courage is one's willingness to take steps forward fearlessly despite the anxiety that may be pulling one back from taking that risk. I began to realize I could now unleash my courage by taking more risks.

Why wouldn't I join that new start-up in the late nineties that I mentioned earlier? What was the worst thing that could have happened? Worst case, I wouldn't rise to the challenge, or the company wouldn't succeed. Regardless, I would have learned a great deal because any type of failure allows us to learn, assuming we employ self-reflection in our routine. The result for me was improved self-esteem and confidence. The company was growing at warp speed. I was accomplishing things I never knew I was capable of. I was hiring people like crazy and learning to manage people. I trusted my instincts. And later, why wouldn't I take the chance to start my consulting business? It was a similar thought pattern and result.

Bottom line, I was starting to take two steps forward for every one step backward, which had been the other way around during my facial reconstructive surgery phase.

I left group meetings feeling more confident in what lay ahead. The numbers around group therapy speak for themselves. In a study published in 2014, researchers analyzed what happened when individuals with depression received group cognitive behavioral therapy. They found that 44 percent of the patients reported significant improvements.[25]

According to the National Library of Medicine, "Group therapy increased the proportion of patients with clinically meaningful improvement post-treatment in comparison with no treatment. [A] study found that 48.2% of patients who participated in group therapy had clinically meaningful improvement post-treatment in comparison to only 18.5% who saw improvement without group therapy."[26]

Practicing Visualization/Guided Imagery

I became a voracious reader in my twenties, and while I was trying to figure out my path forward, I was fortunate to find many books

25   Kendra Cherry, "Group Therapy: Definition, Types, Techniques, and Efficacy," Verywell Mind, November 13, 2023, https://www.verywellmind.com/what-is-group-therapy-2795760.

26   W. McDermut, I.W. Miller, and R.A. Brown, "The Efficacy of Group Psychology for Depression: A Meta-analysis and Review of the Empirical Research," *Database of Abstracts of Reviews of Effects (DARE)*, 2001, https://www.ncbi.nlm.nih.gov/books/NBK68475/.

on the power of visualization and guided imagery. Think of these practices as ways to communicate a goal or message to your brain. Scientific studies have proven there is a connection between what we think and the physical actions we then take.

Guided imagery is probably the most accurate depiction of the practice, but some refer to it as positive imaging or mental imagery. Visualization denotes the visual component, but guided imagery is more powerful because of its multi-sensory approach— it uses your sight, hearing, touch, smell, and taste.

I had practiced guided imagery to some degree in my past, mostly in high school athletics, so it seemed relatively easy to try it out again in a way that I felt could help relieve my anxiety while in the midst of my adversity.

Throughout the course of my diagnosis, treatment, and recovery, I was still required to have CT scans on a regular basis to ensure I didn't have another recurrence of my cancer. Between those CT scans, I often had physical issues that created tremendous anxiety and fear (the tears rolling down my cheeks as I made photocopies at the law firm, scar tissue buildup that felt and looked like tumors, etc.). My nerves and anxiety would reach new levels that I hadn't ever experienced in the past. If meditation and visualization could help relieve some of that anxiety, I was all in for giving it a try.

I began to employ visualization first, whenever I was nervous or anxious about a recurrence or about an upcoming procedure. My method was just to find five to ten minutes during my day to lie down, shut my eyes, and imagine myself being somewhere I enjoyed being, which was always out in nature.

Back in the late eighties and nineties, I used to backpack a fair amount and enjoyed a mix of destinations, including Big Sur near California's central coast, Desolation Wilderness near Lake Tahoe, and the Trinity Alps in Northern California. Because the Trinity Alps had a variety of landscapes and was probably my favorite destination, I often chose to think about backpacking there when I did my visualization exercises to calm myself down and focus on positive energy.

I would imagine myself hiking along a trail, feeling the weight of my heavy backpack on my shoulders. I would imagine the birds chirping and the sight of aspen leaves fluttering in the wind as I passed aspen groves along certain stretches of the trail. Then I would imagine the trail curving past the grove into an opening, and ahead I would picture a majestic, plunging waterfall. I would imagine myself hiking toward the waterfall, removing my backpack, and hiking toward a section that I could stand under without losing my footing or getting washed away. I would imagine the ice cold, crisp, clear, refreshing mountain water careening over my head and face and washing away any negativity, any malignancy, any of my worries. I would imagine the healing water cascading off my head and then flowing down my body and out into the stream. And I would repeat this process over and over again. It always seemed to soothe me and put me at ease.

Boom! In five to ten minutes, I would feel refreshed, energized, and ready to take on the rest of my day.

I did further research on the power of visualization and found there were many studies on the impact it could have on athletic achievement if followed regularly. In *Psycho-Cybernetics*, Maxwell Maltz refers to a study by *Research Quarterly*[27] on the effects of mental practice on improving skill in making basketball free throws.[28] One group practiced shooting free throws every day for twenty days and was scored on day one and day twenty. Another group was scored at the same interval, but did not practice at all. A third group was scored at the same interval but spent twenty minutes per day *imagining* they were shooting the free throws.

---

[27] L. Verdelle Clark, "Effect of Mental Practice on the Development of a Certain Motor Skill," *Research Quarterly* 34(4) (December 1960): 560–569.

[28] Maxwell Maltz, *Psycho-Cybernetics* (New York: TarcherPerigee/Random House, 2015), 40.

The first group improved by 24 percent. The second group showed no improvement. The third group, which only visualized shooting the free throws but did not physically practice, improved by 23 percent.

How amazing is that? According to the study, if a basketball player is not able to make it to an actual basketball court to shoot free throws but can visualize from home instead, they may be able to maintain almost the same level of efficiency as if they practiced twenty days straight.

According to a Russian study in the early eighties that was outlined by the authors of *Peak Performance: Mental Training Techniques of the World's Greatest Athletes*, Soviet Olympic athletes received significant performance benefits from visualization. The athletes were divided into four groups several times a week and tasked with training for hours during those sessions. Each group had a different mix of physical versus mental training.

	Group 1	Group 2	Group 3	Group 4
Physical Training (%)	100	75	50	25
Mental Training (%)	0	25	50	75

The best outcomes were achieved by Group 4, and the less mental training each group had, the worse their performance outcomes were.[29]

According to Logan Christopher, author of the Breaking Muscle article "The History, Science, and How-To of Visualization,"[30] researcher Anne Isaac led a similar experiment with a group of expert and novice trampolinists. She divided the athletes into control groups and experimental groups and tested them on their visualization skills, enabling her to categorize them as either high imagers

---

29   Logan Christopher, "The History, Science, and How-To of Visualization," Breaking Muscle, November 22, 2021, https://breakingmuscle.com/fitness/the-history-science-and-how-to-of -visualization.

30   Ibid.

or low imagers. She then trained each group in three different skills over a six-week period. The training was broken down as follows:

- two and a half minutes of physical practice on the skills
- five minutes of mental imagery for the experimental group
- five minutes of abstract mental problems like math or puzzles for the control group
- two and a half minutes of physical practice once again

The results showed that the high imagers were higher performers than the low imagers.

She also found a significant difference between the control group and the mental imagery group. In the latter group, both the experts and novices saw improvement, demonstrating that visualization works for people whether they are beginners at the practice or more advanced.

Many of us who play golf, myself included, visualize our shot before we hit the ball. We visualize the trajectory of the ball as well as its landing spot.

Obviously, I need to spend more time physically practicing *and* visualizing, because my accuracy based on visualization alone still leaves much to be desired on the golf course. But I'm confident it is helping to some degree, and without doing visualization at all, God knows where my game and index would be.

There is extensive proof of the power of visualization and guided imagery, with findings that are so compelling that I believe everyone should at least try it. According to Leaders.com, 67 percent of people who use visualization experience a boost in confidence, and 76 percent of people who write their goals down actually achieve them.[31] Jim Carrey, Lady Gaga, Beyoncé, Sara Blakely (billionaire founder of SPANX), Michael Jordan, Katie

---

31 Josh Axe, "8 Visualization Strategies That Make Your Goals a Reality," Leaders, May 17, 2023, https://leaders.com/articles/personal-growth/visualization.

Ledecky (ten-time Olympic swimming medalist), and many others credit visualization for their success. Coincidentally, Sara Blakely also has made it a continuing practice for her and her company to embrace failure and learn from it.

According to National Library of Medicine research,[32] the effectiveness of guided imagery in reducing stress and anxiety is significant, with one study showing that twenty minutes of guided imagery significantly reduced anxiety and cortisol levels for those with preoperative anxiety.[33]

Practicing Mindfulness and Meditation

Meditation is another amazing practice that can provide mental clarity and emotional calm. Though I have practiced meditation to some degree, I personally have found visualization/guided imagery easier in terms of focusing on a single activity rather than trying to clear my mind completely. That said, I know lots of people who swear by the benefits of meditation. I did feel better afterward. I was just unable to make it a regular practice I looked forward to.

Visualization/guided imagery is an active exercise, whereas meditation is more of a restful activity. Mindfulness is one form of meditation. In today's world—one in which we experience constant interruptions and are forced to juggle instant messaging, email, and conference calls—mindfulness helps to quiet the mind and is something any of us can incorporate into our day. There are various mindfulness practices, all of which can be added to any of our activities, which is what makes mindfulness so potentially powerful. When you are walking or even involved in a conversation, mindfulness is a perfect way to calm yourself from the noise that fills your day.

---

32 Loren Toussaint et al., "Effectiveness of Progressive Muscle Relaxation, Deep Breathing, and Guided Imagery in Promoting Psychological and Physiological States of Relaxation," *Evidence-Based Complementary and Alternative Medicine*, (July 2021), doi.org/10.1155/2021/5924040.

33 M. Felix et al., "Guided Imagery Relaxation Therapy on Preoperative Anxiety: A Randomized Clinical Trial," *Revista Latino-Americana De Enfermagem* 26 (2018): 3101. doi.org//10.1590/1518-8345.2850.3101.

All mindfulness really requires is that you focus on being intensely aware of what you are feeling and sensing in the moment without trying to interpret or make judgments about whatever that is. As you learn associated breathing methods and other practices, you can relax your body and mind, and at the same time reduce stress. Studies show that mindfulness improves sleep and attention as well.

Mindfulness can be especially helpful if you experience negative self-talk. Step back, take a deep breath, and close your eyes. Try to focus on your breath as it moves in and out of your body. If you have only a minute to do this, you'll find even that little amount of time can help calm you and relieve some of your anxiety and doubts.

I practiced this regularly during my workday. After a confrontational call, I would step back from my desk, take a deep breath, count to five, take another deep breath, and then stand up and walk for thirty seconds or so. I typically felt refreshed before I took on my next task. I was in the right frame of mind for my next conversation or message I had to write.

One thing I've always found about mindfulness is that it enables you to appreciate what you have and be grateful for the present moment. Not unlike what I covered earlier in this book about being attentive, aware, and alert to what's around you, mindfulness is really about paying attention. Like guided imagery, it encourages you to use all your senses—touch, sound, sight, smell, and taste.

I love the distinction that Jon Kabat-Zinn draws in his book *Full Catastrophe Living* when he is talking to a reporter who thinks she has synthesized his concept of living intentionally from moment to moment. The reporter says, "Oh, you mean to live for the moment." "No, it isn't that," replies Kabat-Zinn. "That has a hedonistic ring to it. I mean to live *in* the moment."[34]

---

34 Jon Kabat-Zinn, *Full Catastrophe Living: Using the Wisdom of Your Body and Mind to Face Stress, Pain, and Illness* (New York: Bantam Books, 2013), 5.

Mindfulness can lead to improved reflection as well. You may find that you are rarely if ever fully engaged in your activities (conversation, meals, etc.) because you are thinking about something else or comparing the pizza you are eating to one you had last week. This might seem subtle, but as Kabat-Zinn explains, "If you are only partially conscious over a period of years . . . you may miss some of the most precious experiences of your life, such as connecting with the people you love, or with sunsets or the crisp morning air . . . Why? Because you were 'too busy' and your mind too encumbered with what you *thought* was important in that moment to take the time to stop, to listen, to notice things."[35]

In a 1998 study, Kabat-Zinn collaborated with doctors in the division of dermatology at the University of Massachusetts Medical Center to study people with psoriasis, a skin disease, while they were undergoing ultraviolet light therapy.[36] Psoriasis is a disease that fluctuates but often is exacerbated by emotional stress and other factors. (Incidentally, my wife Sue suffered from it for a period of time when she was undergoing tremendous stress. When that situation mostly resolved itself, her psoriasis disappeared, so I am a firm believer that emotional stress can cause it.)

The standard therapy used to treat psoriasis is ultraviolet light treatment, also known as phototherapy. In the 1998 study, thirty-seven patients who were about to undergo the therapy were divided into two groups. One group of patients practiced mindfulness meditation during therapy, and as the treatment progressed they were encouraged to also practice visualization. The other group received therapy without practicing mindfulness. Those who did practice it saw that their skin cleared four times faster than those in the other group.

There is a cancer-specific, mindfulness-based approach called the Mindfulness-Based Cancer Recovery program, developed by

---

35   Ibid., 11.

36   Ibid., 204–206.

Linda Carlson and Michael Speca at the University of Calgary.[37] Their results point to significant improvements in breast cancer and prostate cancer patients. A one-year follow-up study showed these patients had a higher quality of life, decreased stress, decreased blood pressure, and other improvements.

Kabat-Zinn's own program, Mindfulness-Based Stress Reduction (MBSR), has produced astounding results.[38] According to a study, people with chronic pain who were undergoing training in the MBSR program saw remarkable benefits after eight weeks of practicing meditation at home and attending weekly classes at the hospital. Seventy-two percent of the patients experienced a 33 percent or greater reduction in pain, while 61 percent saw a reduction greater than 50 percent. These same individuals also saw a 30 percent improvement in how much their pain interfered with daily activities and a 55 percent drop in negative mood states. By the end of the program, participants were taking less pain medication and were more active. These improvements were still in place four years later.

When you are incredibly busy during your workday, instead of eating in a rush just to provide yourself with fuel, step away from your desk or task and try to relax. Take the time to enjoy all aspects of your food. Live in the moment and enjoy the simple pleasures of having a free minute to take in your surroundings and appreciate what you see, hear, smell, and taste. And stop beating yourself up. Stop feeling like you aren't doing enough. Accept yourself and treat yourself the way you would a friend, with kindness.

In chapter 11, when I write about how to embrace change, I'll discuss how corporations are recognizing the value of mindfulness and often recommend employees use it to alleviate stress and anxiety. It's been embraced by the military, sports teams, and corporations worldwide.

---

37 Mindfulness-Based Cancer Recovery, https://www.mindfulcancerrecovery.com.

38 Kabat-Zinn, 370–371.

Practicing Yoga

Yoga is another practice that for many has been life-changing. When practiced correctly and consistently, yoga can help you create union between the body, mind, and soul. It combines physical movement with deep breathing, mindfulness, and meditation. Yoga is known to provide wonderful benefits on its own, including the following:

- Stress reduction: 86 percent of people who practice yoga report a reduction in stress.[39]
- Reduced anxiety: On average, yoga decreases anxiety levels by 40 percent.[40]
- Improved balance and flexibility.
- Improved posture and alleviation of back pain.
- Enhanced heart and brain health. According to NetDoctor, only fifteen minutes of daily yoga practice changes the brain's chemistry and boosts mood.[41] And 69 percent of those who regularly practice yoga experience enhanced well-being with respect to temperament and mood.[42]
- Improved sleep and emotional regulation.
- Decreases in depression levels of approximately 50 percent after just three months.[43]

Visualization/guided imagery, meditation, and yoga are all wonderful practices that can improve your physical and mental well-being. In the act phase of ReBAR, try each one and see what

---

39   J.R. Yoginidra, "50 Blissful Yoga Satistics for 2024," Yoga Earth, January 27, 2024, https://yogaearth.com/yoga-research/yoga-statistics.

40   Mirjana Dobric, "35 Mind-Bending Yoga Statistics to Merge Your Body and Soul," Health Careers, February 12, 2020, https://healthcareers.co/yoga-statistics/.

41   Ibid.

42   Yoga Earth, https://yogaearth.com/yoga-research/yoga-statistics.

43   Health Careers, https://healthcareers.co/yoga-statistics/.

works best for you. There is no correct choice, only more options to consider to ensure your best outcomes. Visualization/guided imagery continues to be my go-to practice when I need to find calm, reinforce positivity, and quickly feel refreshed.

BUILD YOUR RESILIENCE MINDSET

Putting the Act Phase into Practice

List and Prioritize Your Challenges

Think about some things you are challenged by or personal fears you have. Don't think of these as goals that you are trying to achieve. You have not addressed these issues yet, so you cannot assign goals to them. You need to clearly define what these challenges are before you can create an action plan and a set of goals. You may come up with many challenges. That's okay.

In your journal or notebook, list these issues and describe any fears that are holding you back from action to resolve those challenges. Refer to chapter 1 for my overview of the different types of adversity, and review the list to see where your issues fall. Are you having financial difficulties? Are you dealing with physical health challenges? Are there emotional, mental, or social issues that you need to address?

Now start prioritizing the list. What is the most pressing issue for you? I acknowledge this may be emotionally difficult for you, but stick with it. Maybe it's a relationship problem that you haven't addressed yet because you hate confrontation. Maybe it's a self-care issue you haven't attended to because you cannot find the time or resources. Maybe you just don't know where to turn. After ranking the challenges to help determine what's most pressing right now, write down the single most important issue you know you need to focus on first. Leave everything else in a separate list for the time being.

This is the time to begin thinking about how you are going to address this most pressing challenge. Give this a lot of thought over a couple of days or even a week, but don't allow it to drag on too long or you'll lose any sense of urgency. Write down any ideas that come to mind. You'll decide which ones to act on in due course.

Set a Start Date and Timeline

Next, create a rough timeline. Get a calendar and begin noting which steps you'll accomplish by what date. Make it very high-level; don't waste time on too many details. The initial steps will drive the next set of actions.

It doesn't matter whether your timeline is two weeks, two months, or two years. When you focus on this goal every day, you will find the effort contributing to progress. And before you know it, you will have made headway toward surmounting a very important roadblock in your life.

Each day going forward, think about how you are spending your time. Focus on how to move your life forward by making the most of the time you have each day. Don't waste it on context activities that don't help you make progress. Focus on getting results—think about what you need to do today to get the results you want tomorrow. You'll begin to feel better and improve your self-esteem and confidence, one day at a time.

Set Goals and Use Visualization/Guided Imagery to Move Forward

In your notebook or journal, write down your new goal, but be sure to specify the steps you need to take to address what's most critical now. Below that, add the rough timeline and include some notes on how you plan to use guided imagery five to ten minutes per day to help you visualize that goal.

What will you concentrate on? What future state do you see yourself in? What is the storyline you'll use for that visualization/guided imagery exercise? Is the goal to:

- relax and alleviate anxiety?

- become more patient with other people?

- strengthen yourself physically?

- overcome an illness or manage your disease?

- improve your willpower?

- find that new job you know you can get?

- find a new outlet you would love to try?

- employ that outlet to relieve anxiety?

By answering these questions, you'll be heading toward a new, more confident self. Why? Because you are investing in yourself, and you are rehearsing for your future success and growth. Practice makes perfect, and that's what guided imagery is all about. By envisioning the achievement of your goal, you'll find your real-world actions will become more and more automatic, helping you achieve the success you desire, as well as happiness and a newfound purpose. Any self-doubt you have will begin to disappear and be replaced by renewed and improved self-esteem.

- Are you focusing on what you can control? What is it that you are focusing on?

- Are you staying focused on your most pressing challenge? What is that challenge?

- Are you employing outlets to relieve any stress you are having? What outlets work best for you? Why?

- Are you using therapy? If yes, how is it helping you better cope?

- Have you figured out if visualization/guided imagery, mindfulness, meditation or yoga help you find better calm and day-to-day results? Is there one thing that works best? How are you incorporating that into your day?

CHAPTER 10

Phase 4: Renew

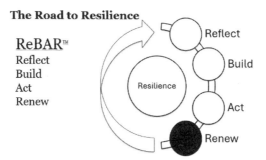

The Road to Resilience

ReBAR™
Reflect
Build
Act
Renew

Reflect

Build

Resilience

Act

Renew

The renew phase is the time in the process to celebrate your successes and reflect on what's working and what's not. What are the things you are acting on that are making your life better? Are there things in your life that aren't helping you that you can do away with? Think of this stage as an opportunity for a refresh so that you continue your recovery more effectively.

When you take time to think about renewing what's working, you are making a commitment to yourself to continue to do the work necessary to improve your life. Remember that my adversity framework is a journey, and in that journey the renew phase requires reinforcement of the actions you take each day. Don't be complacent. Don't start to procrastinate and tell yourself that everything is fine and you don't need to reflect any more.

The renew phase is your reminder to continually reflect and build upon the methods you use to cope so that new challenges become easier for you to tackle. Self-confidence isn't something that is built once; you need to nurture it, and the way to do that is to continue to reflect, adapt, focus on the positive, and take the right actions to move your life forward.

Circumstances will continue to change in life. The renew phase is about reminding yourself what has worked and helped you rebound more effectively. Each new challenge you encounter will be different than the last, but my adversity framework will help increase your chances of success in dealing with any challenge. When you have the right tools in place to succeed, your positive growth mindset can remain solid.

BUILD YOUR RESILIENCE MINDSET

Putting the Renew Phase into Practice

Seek Others to Help You Grow Your Self-Confidence
How can you continue to improve your levels of self-esteem and self-confidence? One method is to focus on surrounding yourself with people who have a positive outlook on life and nurture and support you. Make a note of these go-to people. Describe how they make you feel better.

Make Self-Care a Priority
Keep doing what makes you feel good.

- What is that outlet or hobby that you've always wanted to do, but never made the time for? (For example, learning how to play the guitar or starting to craft again.)

- Stay physically active. Exercise helps to improve your mood—you feel better physically and mentally all day after you exercise. It's worked for me for forty-five years.

- What activities do you enjoy the most?

- Can you find thirty to sixty minutes a day to practice those?

Practice Positive Self-Talk
Remind yourself about things you excel at.

- What are your strengths?

- What special skills and traits do you bring to the table that make you successful at those things?

Practice Gratitude
Be grateful for all that you have. Ponder and reflect or start a gratitude journal.

- What are you grateful for?

- Who are you grateful for?

- Why are you grateful for those people and things?

Get Rid of Negativity

Challenge negative thoughts. Try to switch your thinking to positive self-talk. There is always an inverse to negative thought.

- Are you having negative thoughts?

- What are they?

- How can you turn those negative thoughts into something positive?

Celebrate Your Wins

Remember to celebrate whatever you accomplish. Take the time to reflect on how you were able to achieve that. Build muscle memory from it.

- What are your latest accomplishments?

- How did you achieve them?

- What can you do to be sure you don't lose what you gained from those accomplishments?

Each of these practices will help you improve your self-esteem and confidence and get you one step closer to happiness and fulfillment.

A RECAP, A REQUEST, AND WHAT'S NEXT

The ReBAR framework is designed to help you become more resilient and take life to new heights. It's about finding fulfillment, happiness, success, and purpose.

I ask you to revisit your answers to the questions earlier in this chapter. When you renew, you reflect. You are prepared to face new challenges. The reality of our world is that adversity is ever-present and the way we respond to it defines who we are.

It defined me. But my story has one more chapter. Change is a form of adversity we deal with every day.

CHAPTER 11

Embrace Change— Don't Fear It

W hy is it such a natural human tendency to associate change with adversity? When change is on the horizon, we default to becoming anxious and worried. We fear the unknown, which could bless us as easily as bring challenges our way. We need to embrace change and deal with adversity when it happens. After all, adversity is just part of everyday life.

Self-talk plays a huge role in how we look at change. Some are convinced by their negative self-talk that they are unlucky or have fallen under a dark cloud, or that life just isn't fair.

Others will focus on responding to change in ways that enable them to grow. A challenge is an opportunity to express our best self. We stand to learn from overcoming challenges—for example, about our own strengths and patterns of behavior, information that will help us in the future.

For me, change is exciting. It can be exhilarating to think about life's possibilities when change is the driver of opportunity. Thinking about the future and the unknowns associated with it gives me energy.

As much as many of us may like the idea of stability, calm, and consistency in our lives, change allows us to look at life with a new perspective. In part 3, you'll read stories from people who have overcome tremendous adversity and come out the other side grateful for their experience, as I am for mine. They would never trade that experience for anything.

Change in your life doesn't necessarily mean something catastrophic. It can be little things that require you to make adjustments to your routine, whether that is taking care of an aged parent, picking up your daughter from her first day at elementary school, switching jobs, or finally having the courage to say "no" to someone who directs negative energy your way. Some of those changes may be tough; others you may find liberating.

If you reflect regularly and take stock of those little changes in our day-to-day lives, you will realize that change isn't so bad. You will also be prepared for larger changes to come. As you adjust to these changes—because you must—realize that nine times out of ten, the change isn't really a big deal. If anything, we learn from each one and can find blessings in each of them. Dr. Bernie Siegel, who reviewed my book *At Face Value: My Triumph Over a Disfiguring Cancer*, said, "Anyone who needs to see that there are blessings in every curse should read Healey's book and learn from his experience about how to create a healing team and how to heal one's own life."

By picking up your daughter from school, you can spend more quality time with her. By taking care of an aged parent, you become grateful you can give back to the person who helped you become the person you are. By saying "no" to the person who brings negative energy to your life, you realize you have invested in yourself and your happiness. You can be grateful for that too.

According to a study dating back to the sixties, Drs. Thomas Holmes and Richard Rahe of the University of Washington Medical School found that life changes can predispose a person to illness.[44] So having the tools at your disposal to address change as you encounter it (such as a framework like ReBAR) can make all the difference in whether that change leads to illness. Make

---

44   Jon Kabat-Zinn, *Full Catastrophe Living: Using the Wisdom of Your Body and Mind to Face Stress, Pain, and Illness* (New York: Bantam Books, 2013), 302–303.

it a practice to prepare, reflect, and act with positivity. Change often exists outside your control; however, how you respond to it is completely within your control.

A DOUBLE WHAMMY: TECHNOLOGY AND THE COVID-19 PANDEMIC

Technology provides an excellent perspective on change. I spent my entire career in the high-tech industry, mostly in a marketing and sales leadership capacity. I worked in all parts of the high-tech supply chain, from distribution to systems integration, software, hardware, and services. I cannot remember a time when each segment of that industry wasn't undergoing major change—whether that was consolidation, margin compression from competition, or new disrupters focused on changing the game with technological innovation.

When I look back on my career, I'm reminded of one thing in particular. Each disruption or change improved the industry, made it more efficient, and led to higher levels of customer satisfaction and success in the process. During my last decade in the industry, I focused on communicating the value of digital transformation to customers and prospects. At the root of digital transformation is change.

Digital transformation is about digitizing business processes to help transform the business. Operational and financial methods can be optimized while costs and risks can be minimized. One benefit of the COVID-19 pandemic was that digital transformation was turbocharged. For knowledge workers to continue to be productive, businesses had to enable secure work-from-home environments that mirrored in-office work. Remote work solutions proliferated because of technologies for online collaboration, such as Cisco Webex and Zoom.

Despite COVID-19 being incredibly disruptive to our daily lives, few knowledge workers lost their jobs during the pandemic.

But if you were in the services sector (restaurants, hotels, etc.) you were displaced and left without a job overnight. If you were a healthcare worker, you were often tasked to work longer and harder and forced to take health risks that so many others weren't because you were in the belly of the pandemic beast.

And it wasn't just about work and life changes. For many, the COVID-19 pandemic created emotional and mental distress that we'll be addressing for years to come. Children lost critical time from in-school activities, and social development was impacted in ways we're still learning from. Mentoring and team-building were largely abandoned for three-plus years as early and mid-career professionals were limited to virtual meetings and discussions, losing the ability to communicate face-to-face.

As COVID-19 faded into the background, businesses were keen to bring their employees back to the office. Business and digital transformation continued at another level as staff returned to the workplace.

> As businesses continue to adapt to the aftermath of the COVID-19 pandemic, I am grateful that I can play a meaningful role by presenting my story and the tools I've learned to use in my own life to help others cope with challenges they are facing. I am thrilled that corporations have made mental health a big priority within their organizations, and that the stigma on mental health isn't nearly what it used to be.

ARTIFICIAL INTELLIGENCE (AI) IS JUST ONE EXAMPLE OF HOW TECHNOLOGY IS RESHAPING OUR WORLD

Because Wall Street never stops evaluating the earnings picture of companies, new digital trends continue to emerge that address additional cost controls, new revenue models, improved customer experience, and the risks from cyberattacks. But guess what? When you minimize costs and reorganize around new initiatives, people fear they'll lose their jobs—and sometimes they do.

Network automation is one example that a network engineer might be threatened by, for example. Network engineers may perceive that new automated processes will replace the programming and scripts they currently write and the job they get paid to do. The reality is these engineers will typically retain their jobs and become tasked with more strategic priorities if and when a network automation solution is deployed, whether that is to automate operating system upgrades or identify and remediate configuration drift. Network engineers oftentimes end up with more strategic positions within their companies, where they can provide greater business impact and value.

Artificial intelligence (AI) and one of its main subsets, machine learning, are just two current megatrends in business transformation. I'm an optimist and believe that with AI, we'll end up creating more jobs and eliminating tasks so that the workforce is freed up to do more creative and strategic work in the long term. Benefits will accrue to society instead of creating setbacks as many people fear.

According to the management consulting firm McKinsey, generative AI's financial impact will top $2.6 trillion annually. That's bigger than the entire U.S. e-commerce market and 4.5 times bigger than the entire cloud computing market. Entrepreneur Mark Cuban has said many times that AI will have far-reaching impact immeasurably beyond the internet and current technologies.

In an interview at the World Economic Forum in winter 2024, Microsoft cofounder Bill Gates said that with artificial intelligence for coders, "you're seeing 40% to 50% productivity improvements, which means you can get programs [done] sooner. You can make them higher quality and make them better. So mostly what we'll see is that the productivity of white-collar [workers] will go up."[45]

Without a doubt, AI will change the workforce. It will allow us to streamline processes and improve efficiency. If the chart below is indicative of what's coming, all of us need to equip ourselves the best we can to adapt.

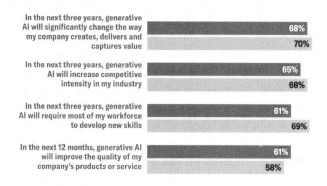

AI IS CHANGING THE COMPETITIVE LANDSCAPE

● U.S. CEOs ● CEOs GLOBALLY

In the next three years, generative AI will significantly change the way my company creates, delivers and captures value
68%
70%

In the next three years, generative AI will increase competitive intensity in my industry
65%
68%

In the next three years, generative AI will require most of my workforce to develop new skills
61%
69%

In the next 12 months, generative AI will improve the quality of my company's products or service
61%
58%

SOURCE: PWC'S 27TH ANNUAL GLOBAL CEO SURVEY, WHICH SURVEYS 4700+ CEOS ACROSS 105 COUNTRIES AND TERRITORIES.

yahoo/finance

Orgvue, a UK-based organizational design and workplace planning platform, reported in October 2023 that "generative AI will transform 40% of all working hours within the next decade, while . . . 40% of enterprise applications will have AI built in by 2024."[46]

45 Brian Sozzi, "Microsoft Co-founder Bill Gates on AI's Impact on Jobs: It's Great for White-Collar Workers, Coders," Yahoo Finance, January 16, 2024, https://finance.yahoo.com/news/microsoft-co-founder-bill-gates-on-ais-impact-on-jobs-its-great-for-white-collar-workers-coders-110005579.html?.tsrc=372.

46 "AI and Its Impact on Workforce Transformation," Orgvue, October 31, 2023, https://www.orgvue.com/resource/articles/ai-and-its-impact-on-workforce-transformation.

What's essential for providers of digital business transformation capabilities and generative AI is that when selling their products and services, they must focus their value propositions on the business outcomes (increased revenue and customer satisfaction, reduced costs) that their solutions will provide. That should be their focus, not the potential workforce reduction from streamlined business processes. Their customers want to focus on growth, not on contraction. Business contraction is not the initiative a chief information officer (CIO) wants to bring to the CEO. If it is a byproduct, that may be acceptable.

The information technology decision-makers these providers of digital transformation capabilities engage with (the CIO, VP of information technology, or director of information technology) may fear proposing a transformative digital solution to their leadership because it could mean they'll lose their own jobs if implementation of that solution goes awry, takes longer than anticipated, or delivers results that are below expectations. The average tenure of a CIO in today's Fortune 1000 companies is in the range of eighteen months. A cyberattack or failed software implementation could cost them their job.

Regardless, when decisions are made to protect jobs rather than drive innovation, it tends to be a losing battle in the long term. Change and progress are inevitable, and the learnings gained from them are always superior to resistance—for both the business and the employee.

Overall, most of the technology implementations we delivered for our customers provided improvements to the business, demonstrated a return on investment, and enhanced customer experience. And the companies creating these solutions are generating a tremendous number of new jobs and opportunities that will challenge workers to learn new skills. That's progress. That's more opportunity, not less.

The companies delivering business transformation solutions are name-brand organizations. They are the ones enabling the transformation in the business-to-consumer space as well as business-to-business (think Netflix, Amazon, Microsoft, Nvidia, Alphabet/Google, Adobe Systems, ServiceNow, Cisco Systems, McKinsey, Accenture, Deloitte), and without them we wouldn't be able to live, play, and work the way we do today.

These change agents are making each of us more efficient, more productive, and able to enjoy and digitally capture our everyday life experiences in ways never before possible. Think about how easy it is today to stream movies and shows without getting off our couches at home. Ponder how wonderful it is that you don't have to leave your home to buy clothes, electronics, food, or any number of other things. You can order online in seconds and have it delivered the same or next day.

And on the business-to-business side, consider how revolutionary ServiceNow's business model has become. ServiceNow (NYSE: NOW) is a software company that helps businesses replace manual processes with efficient digital workflows that improve employee productivity. The company's Now Platform includes modules that help IT professionals accelerate digital transformation efforts, rank-and-file employees automate common tasks, creative professionals build apps using low-code programming and hyper-automation tools, and customer service and sales professionals interact more effectively with their clients.[47]

These examples show how transformational technology has become in our day-to-day work and personal lives, and they demonstrate that all of these changes improve our lives by simplifying how we complete tasks, allowing us to find more time for new endeavors and goals we would like to achieve.

In all these businesses and so many others, digital disruption drives long-term growth. But no one within these organizations is spared the impact of the changes taking place. It's not uncommon for organizations like these to experience regular reorganizations

---

47   "Buy ServiceNow As It Cashes In on Ambitious AI Aspirations," The Motley Fool, January 2024.

that require many of the employees to change their jobs every year. According to the U.S. Bureau of Labor Statistics, "management analytics," which includes change management, is projected to grow by 14 percent from 2018 to 2028.

As reported in Prosci's *Best Practices in Change Management*, twelfth edition, when workers were asked to identify the leading causes of change within their organizations, technology and digital transformation was by far the most common response:

- technology and digital transformation (37%)
- regulatory changes and compliance (9%)
- environmental sustainability and climate change (9%)
- talent retention and turnover (9%)
- cultural and organizational change (9%)[48]

One lesson I learned early in my career is that at least within the business world, we shouldn't think about change as something we associate with new challenges, but frame it as an opportunity. Change in business is never made for its own sake. Change is always driven by new innovative ideas that can drive revenue, increase customer satisfaction and retention, and a host of other things.

BUILD YOUR RESILIENCE MINDSET

Framing Change as Opportunity

Turning things upside down or thinking outside the box as a business or an individual contributor can often become the golden path to success. And if you can make a habit out of daily reflection, you may just find that you can be the one to drive new

---

48   Tim Creasey, "Change Management Trends Outlook: 2024 and Beyond," Prosci, January 9, 2025, https://www.prosci.com/blog/change-management-trends-2024-and-beyond.

innovations and be the beneficiary of change, rather than the one who fears it.

Being adaptable and resilient will bring you more opportunities in your work life and greater happiness in your personal life. And if you get to a position where you're recognized as a problem solver, you'll begin to build your personal brand, and those around you will associate you with progress. You'll rise to new heights within your organization, and that will give you newfound confidence you never knew you'd be capable of having.

That confidence will help you to take more risks, and though that may take you out of your comfort zone, that's exactly how you will grow as a person and as a leader. Remember, taking a risk means you might not realize the optimal outcome, but that is not a definition of failure. It's a definition of progress. Lessons learned will help you succeed in your next endeavor.

Embrace change when confronted with it. Think of the benefits of progress. And put the ReBAR framework to work—use the tools and exercises from this book, reflect on the change as it's taking place, and embrace it to create your future self! Here are some questions to get you started with reflecting on your relationship with change.

- Reflect back over the past year and think about what little changes you have made. Do you have a new routine that is now part of your daily life? Did you choose to incorporate that new routine into your life (a new outlet, a regular meeting you now have with your mentor), or was it something that came up that you were forced to take on (taking your daughter to school every day, caring for an aged parent, doing more of the family chores to do your fair share)?

- Do you feel these little changes give you more purpose and make you feel lighter about life? Or does it stress you out? Think about the silver linings of these changes to your routine. There must be some.

- Have there been changes in your professional life that have changed your routine? A new boss? Maybe it's a new strategic plan that you need to focus on.

- Are you now required to reduce the number of days you work from home? Does that stress you out?

- Do you worry about future changes in your work environment? A reorganization? Are you spending time anticipating what those changes will look like and how they'll affect you? Can you control that?

- Are you excited by the possibilities of a reorganization in your company? Do you embrace change and find it exciting?

PART 3

Limitless Possibilities

CHAPTER 12

True Inspiration

P art 3 is about heroes and people I like to call my idols because
each of them helps me put life in perspective and inspires
me to live with purpose and positivity. Your own story can look
like this too. Let's learn how.

Do we wish our adversities on others? No. Can we learn to
cope with adversity, and ultimately to thrive? Hopefully. Will we
gain wisdom and realize our opportunities are still limitless? Yes.
Can we rebuild our confidence, or build it for the first time? YES!

I don't believe my story is unique. Sure, the circumstances
related to my facial difference are uncommon, but what I learned
about life during my adversity, and the gifts my adversity provided
me, are common. There are so many others who have overcome
tremendous obstacles—far more challenging than my own—
and have come out of those experiences appreciative, grateful,
and often with newfound purpose. They realized that whatever
happened to them was not the worst thing possible, but a gift
in disguise.

There are countless others who inspire me and remind me of
the resilience of the human spirit and the unbelievable strength
we can find to not just recover from adversity, but to thrive.

In the pages that follow, I am going to dig into the lives of
seven people who have overcome tremendous adversity, share

the tools they employed to power through their challenges, and conclude with where they are today. I promise that you will be inspired by their stories and humbled by their experiences.

ROBERT PAYLOR

L like me, Robert went to UC Berkeley ("Cal"). Like me, he was living his life on Easy Street until a single moment changed his life forever. A true competitor, strong and elite athlete, and born leader, Robert was competing for the collegiate rugby national championship with his Cal teammates on May 6, 2017. He took a hard tackle and suffered a spinal cord injury. He was told he would never walk or move his hands again.

That was not Robert's way. Through his relentless determination he defied the odds. He went on to graduate from UC Berkeley, powering himself across the stage to receive his diploma at the Greek Theater. Today he is making progress in his fight to walk again.

When I spoke to Robert on January 17, 2024, he told me it was the 2,447th day since his injury. When I asked him why tracking the number of days was important to him, his response was something all of us should think about as we go about our day-to-day lives. "Tracking my days helps ensure I am intentional with every day."

As I write this book in 2024, Robert is still in a wheelchair, but he is now walking four hundred yards around his house every day.

That's roughly one lap around a track, an incredible achievement for someone who had been told only six and a half years earlier that he'd never walk again.

While the nature of his adversity and journey are different from mine, he told me my ReBAR framework had similar elements to his own regimen for healing and recovery. Reflecting and building phases were critical to Robert for maintaining a positive outlook and preparing to face the unthinkable and persevere, as were his support system (not spending a single moment alone during his initial recovery), having trust in his medical professionals, and his faith.

Robert's reflections in his hospital room reminded him to never lose sight of all he learned from childhood to adulthood, and he drew strength from how he prepared for success as a young man.

He especially credits two key aspects of reflection that hearkened back to his childhood and which have remained with him throughout his life.

Athletics and Team Sports

As a graduate of Jesuit High School in Carmichael, California (outside of Sacramento), Robert was a member of the most successful high school rugby program in the United States, a school with eleven national championships to its credit. He went on to Cal, which has won thirty-three collegiate rugby national championships, including one on that fateful day in May 2017. He credits athletics with giving him the resilience and discipline that became core to him. Training was constant, committing to your teammates was required, accountability was paramount, and if he wasn't sore every day, he was, in his own words, "pissed off."

Using the discipline of reflection, usually during the quiet hours at night in his hospital room, he conjured up his competitive spirit to "knuckle down and do the work" that had to be done if he was going to improve his situation—to be able to breathe on his own, move his hands, and feed himself again. It was hard not to get lost in the spiral of depression. He often woke up in tears. But he remembered what made him strong, what made him the best version of himself up to the day of his accident. Grit. Determination. Focus. Fight.

In Robert's case, competing in athletics is what taught him how to be the best version of himself, and that experience and the learnings he gained from it will live on in his spirit forever. Athletics provided the foundation that gives Rob the courage and strength to work hard each day.

Faith and a Turning Point

Robert's faith also played a powerful role in his recovery. He reflected on his life's purpose, knowing his faith would help him find his way. He realized he could accept what happened to him and share what he learned as gifts to so many others.

Robert wouldn't wish what happened to him on anyone, but he spent a lot of time reflecting and thinking about his vision, his goal. His singular goal was to walk again and become wheelchair-independent. He never lost hope and makes incredible strides every day because he remains committed to that goal, as well as to a newfound purpose of using his experience to help others.

He shared a key turning point in his life with me, one that taught him to have more empathy and to look outside himself. He decided to go on a journey to visit the Sanctuary of Our Lady of Lourdes in France, a pilgrimage for the sick and disabled, known for miraculous healings. On his thirteen-hour flight from Los Angeles to Lourdes, he prayed and cried the entire time.

He arrived at the site and experienced immersion in Lourdes's water. Though he wasn't miraculously healed, the experience was life-changing. Even though Robert was a quadriplegic and felt his situation was dire, he met others who had stage 4 cancer, ALS, and other diseases that were terminal. These people told him they just wanted more time, and he realized at that point he would never complain again. He had a newfound perspective and is now even more empathetic than before. "Empathy and perspective," he told me, "are the key to happiness."

Robert's message is powerful. He speaks across the U.S. now, inspiring thousands. He is also writing a book. He explained to me that all of us are paralyzed by something, whether it be physical, mental, or emotional. Through his book and speaking, his purpose is to help others overcome their challenges by identifying their adversity, making a plan, and acting on it to defeat whatever paralyzes them.[49]

For more information or to contact Robert, visit RobertPaylor .com.

---

49 Author interview with Robert Paylor on January 17, 2024, and website content from http://www .robertpaylor.com.

CAPTAIN CHARLIE PLUMB

I was both inspired and incredibly humbled by Charlie's story when I first heard it. I was dumbfounded by how someone could not only survive but ultimately thrive after being a prisoner of war (POW) in Vietnam for 2,103 days, only to return home and be confronted with even more adversity.

Not surprisingly, the tools and methods Charlie depended upon during his ordeal are not unlike my own, and strikingly similar to Robert Paylor's as well.

I grew up across the street from another Vietnam POW, but his path was very different than Charlie's. A POW for almost two thousand days, he was a man with a broken spirit who struggled every day of his life upon his return home. No judgment from me. I cannot imagine how much suffering he endured during his six years of confinement.

What made these two men's responses so different? We'll never know exactly, but Charlie relied on foundational tools he learned as a child, similar again to mine and Robert Paylor's.

Captain Charlie Plumb was a graduate of the Naval Academy at Annapolis. He went on to fly the F-4 Phantom jet and was a Top Gun fighter pilot, but on his seventy-fifth mission, only five days before he was to return home to the U.S., he was shot down over enemy territory, captured, and tortured. He was imprisoned in an eight-foot-by-eight-foot cell. The survival courses he took before shipping off to Vietnam—Survival, Evasion, Resistance, and Escape (SERE)—did not adequately prepare him for his eventual capture and the isolation he would have to endure to survive. True survival required that he tap into his foundational learnings from childhood and the communal support of his fellow POWs.

What prepared him the most for those six years of confinement were the lessons he learned from his mother and father. His mother was a devout Christian and practiced forgiveness, something most of us struggle with throughout life. Charlie remembers ejecting from his jet upon impact by a surface-to-air missile, viewing his remote surroundings, and then taking a deep breath and praying he would have "the guts it was going to take to survive" the harrowing ordeal he knew was ahead of him. He didn't panic under pressure. He made a choice to pray to be given the strength he needed.

Like me, he relied heavily on the practice of reflection. It took three to four months of deep thought for Charlie to figure out what his survival tactics would be. But reflection came surprisingly easy to him. In the darkness of solitary confinement, very few things impacted his senses, freeing him of distractions and enabling him to focus on the end goal of being freed. Focus, faith, and positivity would become his building blocks for survival.

He credits his father for teaching him about discipline. Being disciplined in his approach to survival and keeping his faith in God gave him the essential tools to get up every morning with a purpose. Charlie's faith and discipline were wired into him before he was shot down.

From there his first major step was to forgive his captors, freeing him of bitterness, resentment, negative self-talk, anger, and blame. Then, over time, Charlie and the other POWs worked more and more as a team, and a leadership structure was created whereby communication became essential to survival and positivity. Their communication system consisted of tugging on a wire between prison cells. It was a kind of Morse code. With teamwork as the foundation of this newfound support group, each POW developed a purpose of keeping faith and hoping for survival and their collective release from the prison camp. Charlie was quickly able to distinguish himself as a professional in underground communications and even served as the camp chaplain for two years.

From my interview with Charlie, I can attest to how his positivity is incredibly contagious. When you speak with him, it feels like you're talking to an old friend. There's enormous honesty and vulnerability.

For example, he emphasizes how adversity is a terrible thing to waste. That might sound pretty odd. But Charlie recounts how only three months before his release from the prison camp, his wife filed for divorce. He was shocked to find this out upon coming home. His resilience, having been tested to the breaking point in a POW camp, was now being tested again. Charlie's response was remarkable. He was quick to forgive her, freeing himself of any bitterness, and he understood that she didn't have the benefit of a support group like he did in the camp. Nor did she have the benefit of even knowing whether Charlie was alive. He understood that she needed to move on with her life and build a family. He didn't question what happened, but had faith that he would find his way to build a life as a free man.

Upon Charlie's return to the U.S., finding a new purpose wasn't a struggle. He began speaking to audiences and then wrote a memoir. Still, people had questions and continued asking him to present to their own groups, associations, and companies. He has now spoken to many thousands since his return who have no doubt been inspired to find ways to overcome their challenges.

Charlie's military honors include two Purple Hearts, the Legion of Merit, the Silver Star, the Bronze Star, and the POW Medal.[50]

For more information and to contact Captain Charlie Plumb, visit CharliePlumb.com.

---

50 Author interview with Charlie Plumb on January 26, 2024, and website content from http://www .charlieplumb.com.

SHAWN HARPER

I stumbled across Shawn Harper's story and was struck by how he defined himself as "uniquely enabled," a man focused on the abundance he has been blessed with, not the shortcomings that others tried to define him by as a youth.

As a young boy, Shawn had multiple learning disabilities, including severe dyslexia. He encountered bullying—people called him stupid and told him he'd never make it in life. But Shawn believed in himself and his dream, which was to find a way to complete his education and play in the NFL.

School was never easy for Shawn, but he learned to cope, and his unending faith in God was instrumental in the courage he was able to find to remain optimistic about pursuing his dream.

Graduating last in his high school class with a 1.62 GPA, and voted most likely to fail, Shawn didn't let that stop him. He knew that to get to the NFL, he needed to prove himself in football at the next level. As he focused on his goal, Shawn knew he'd never get "cured" of his learning disabilities. He believed he was chosen for a purpose, though, and fought his way through on the field and the classroom.

Shawn learned by being able to listen, a skill he mastered by listening with his eyes, as he describes it. He believes he is uniquely enabled to see what others don't see and hear what they don't hear.

In community college, he struggled, but his work ethic and grit enabled him to make his way to Indiana University, where his listening skills allowed him to learn at the level he needed to get his degree. Before Shawn knew it, he was drafted into the NFL. Not only did he become an offensive lineman with the Los Angeles Rams, Tennessee Titans, Indianapolis Colts, and NFL Europe, but he became the CEO of a successful security company as well.

That's overcoming adversity in a major way and a testament to learning to embrace your abilities.

Preparation and hard work are at the root of Shawn's success. He too had and continues to be blessed with an incredible support system at home, a positive attitude, and a strong faith, which combined enable him to face new challenges.

When I asked Shawn if he has found greater happiness because of what he had to overcome, he answered with an emphatic "Yes!", but he believes that happiness stems from his blessing from God. After the NFL, he was blessed to find a new purpose: to become mission-minded and help young people who were struggling with their own challenges. Shawn not only delivers his inspirational message to youths, but as a highly regarded entrepreneur he has the ear and respect of business leaders across his home state of Ohio and the country.

When Shawn was told he was stupid and would never make it, he was able to prove the naysayers wrong. Throughout his life, he has continued to inspire everyone to pursue their own dreams. When he speaks to students, he empowers them to write their own destiny by figuring out what challenges they need to overcome so that they too can develop what he calls the Winner's Mindset.

Like me, Shawn is grateful for what he overcame and uses reflection to continue to find more self-insight and growth.

Instead of calling it "reflection," though, Shawn likes to think about what his "wins" were that day. What did he learn? Who did he meet? How is he more grateful today? What is he grateful for? Who will he be able to help tomorrow?

Shawn found his calling. His adversity gave him an ability to think differently and to use tools that make him "uniquely enabled" and not disabled.[51]

For more information and to contact Shawn Harper, visit ShawnSpeaks.com.

---

[51] Author interview with Shawn Harper on February 1, 2024, and website content from http://www .shawnspeaks.com.

SANDY
PRETO

I was lucky to meet Sandy when we worked together at a fast-growing high-tech start-up in the late nineties. I was struck by Sandy's tremendous energy and can-do attitude. She was (and still is) highly creative, blessed with a high degree of enthusiasm, and exceedingly passionate about life.

After I left the company to start my own consulting business, Sandy and I stayed in touch, partly because we had many friends in common, and partly because we would end up having something far more important in common.

About ten years after we worked together, Sandy was diagnosed with stage 3 breast cancer (invasive lobular carcinoma). Her right breast and lymph nodes from her right arm were removed. She underwent chemotherapy and radiation therapy. The stress of her illness was coupled with trying to be a good mom to her three young children and ensuring them she would be okay. None of it was easy.

Upon completion of Sandy's treatment, her partner, Mark Carlton (coincidentally, a close friend of mine who I had worked with in a prior company), threw an "End of Cancer" surprise celebration for Sandy that included hundreds of friends who danced the night away to the music of Luce, a local San Francisco band. The event was electric, and I could tell Sandy and Mark were in their element.

Mark and Sandy knew after Sandy's experience that they wanted to help others struggling with breast cancer, and the way forward was to bring higher awareness of lifestyle, diet, and integrated therapies to the community. The End of Cancer celebration had hit a chord with the two of them, and they knew they could create a special way of making their ambition a reality.

They embarked on creating an education nonprofit to raise awareness for breast cancer research and prevention, but instead of inviting potential donors to traditional fundraisers—galas, 10K runs, golf tournaments, etc.—they chose to bring music and live performances to the forefront of everything they did. The events they hosted were met with energy, enthusiasm, and support from the East Bay community.

But Sandy's journey was far from over. Several months after her celebration, she elected to have her left breast, ovaries, and fallopian tubes removed as a preventative measure. Several months after that, Sandy developed an infection that necessitated removal of her tissue expander. The pathological results indicated she had mold! After five months taking anti-fungal medication to eradicate the mold, she was finally cleared for reconstruction.

Fortunately, Sandy was able to cope and endure her struggle. Her foundational positive approach to life, penchant for living in the moment, and diligent preparation to face what lay ahead allowed her to fall back on a multitude of ways to keep living a full life. It took cancer for the light bulb to come on, but Sandy quickly built a support team to get her through the darkest moments. Her knowledge of and commitment to nutrition was something already essential to her routine, so she continued to learn more to optimize her progress toward recovery.

As an extrovert, she found it easy to let others into her life. Her fearless nature, ability to ask others for help whenever she needed it, and perseverance in continuing to be a great mother to her children gave her the tools she needed to keep moving forward, and her goal was to help others, even in the darkest recesses of her ordeal.

Motivation and action became second nature to Sandy. She focused on living each day with purpose and gained tremendous life perspective by reminding herself to look at the big picture and not focus on the small stuff. She credits this perspective with helping her evolve as a parent and friend to her growing children, who began to experience their own adversities growing up. She practiced meditation and yoga. She did group and individual therapy. Her spirit shone throughout her journey, and she became an inspiration to everyone around her, including her children.

Like me, Sandy is grateful for her experience with cancer. Now a survivor for twelve-plus years, she says cancer has been a gift to her. She is dedicated to educating others and bringing the healing power and unifying nature of music to everyone. Her Notes4Hope nonprofit brings energy and joy to so many. And being a survivor, Sandy wants to help other women with breast cancer in their own day-to-day fights by offering her Wellness and Recovery (WAR) Kits, complete with cancer tips, warm socks, tea, lotions, oils, candles, and many more nurturing items.

Sandy makes reflection a part of her daily routine as well, which reminds her to always be intentional. She has watched her children grow up to become independent, kind, and empathetic adults. Reflection has allowed her to be more at peace than ever before, and she believes she is more empathetic because of her experience with cancer.

One thing I know for sure is that being at a Notes4Hope event helps me reflect. I experience the energy around me and watch the joy music is bringing to everyone in attendance. It sends chills up my spine and reminds me that we should all do our best every day to do our little part in bringing joy to everyone around us.[52]

For more information and to contact Sandy Preto, visit Notes4Hope.org.

---

52 Author interview with Sandy Preto on February 9, 2024, and website content from http://www .notes4hope.org.

LIZA
PAVLAKOS

W hen I first learned about Liza Pavlakos's story, I felt compelled to re-read her bio multiple times. Was it possible for someone to experience so much adversity year after year at such a young age and somehow come out of it not only whole but optimistic, charismatic, successful, and so full of purpose?

Liza grew up in Melbourne, Australia, in an affluent family, but with that "privilege" came a price that is truly incomprehensible. Her parents were so consumed by their careers that Liza garnered little of their attention. At first, you might assume she became unmanageable, spoiled, and entitled because of her freedom. Far from it. When she was only six years old, her uncle began to sexually abuse her and continued to do so for the next two years. At fourteen, she was raped by a cousin. There were no consequences for her offenders. Then her father began to physically abuse her. She became depressed and saw no way out of her situation. She had become a hopeless young girl.

At sixteen, she found the courage to run away from home and began living on the streets of Melbourne. Too young to find her way, she sought out love to fill the void in her life. Unfortunately for Liza, her new boyfriend manipulated her and began physically abusing her. She eventually suffered a broken cheekbone that required extensive reconstruction. Deep in a spiral, she attempted suicide many times.

Finding a semblance of hope, she decided to enroll in school to create more opportunities for herself. But at nineteen, she was kidnapped and assaulted by a stranger who threatened to murder her. Her depression, loneliness, and isolation mounted, even as she was somehow able to free herself from yet another horrible and life-threatening situation. Because she had no self-esteem, she sought out the man who broke her cheekbone because there was no one else to turn to. She became pregnant, and after her son Adam was born, her "boyfriend" continued to assault her in front of her son.

Adam was her sole concern and purpose, so she found a way to escape from her boyfriend one evening to save her son from an abusive home.

She started to make new life choices and began to realize that as a mother she had to protect her child and find a way to get food, shelter, and safety. Her resilience was unmatched. She came up with an idea to empower other young women like herself and was able to organize and launch a beauty pageant, which to Liza became a symbol of her newfound freedom. It was a resounding success. Approximately four thousand people attended the event, and she managed to make a large profit. It would become the first Miss India International beauty pageant in Australia, and that became the catalyst for Liza to begin to believe in herself and realize she had the tenacity to rise from the ashes and build her own life.

From there, Liza took over a failing café in the heart of Melbourne and turned it into a success. She parlayed that into expanding a tailoring business with her new husband from just one location to five and began building inroads with star performers as some of her key clients. She became the mother of five.

But gnawing at her was a desire to do more. Fortunately, Liza had started to make more considered choices, but it was her self-discipline and survival instincts that paved the way to achieving new and audacious goals. With renewed confidence and a focus on self-care—including improving work-life balance— she began to build her path to happiness and purpose. Reflection played a huge role in discovering what fulfillment and success looked like.

She became a keynote speaker, which quickly became her passion, enabling her to share her survival story and make an impact on so many others struggling with their own adversities. Knowing firsthand that healing is a lifelong journey, Liza launched the Mind Hub Directory, a one-stop solution to help those in need find the right mental health practitioner to support them.

As a survivor of PTSD herself, Liza has built her own PTSD framework for recovery that helps her find inner peace and reminds her of where she has come from. In her framework PTSD stands for Purpose, Trust, Success, and Discover. She has certainly found her life Purpose with keynote speaking and Mind Hub, her faith and Trust in the miracle of God, her Success from finding inner peace and purpose, and her growth and continual learning represents Discover.[53] There will be much more to come from Liza—I promise.

For more information and to contact Liza Pavlakos, visit MindHubDirectory.com and LizaPavlakos.com.

---

53   Author interview with Liza Pavlakos on February 20, 2024, and website content from http://www .mindhubdirectory.com.

JAMIE
MoCRAZY

Jamie was twenty-two years old and at the top of her game as a professional slopestyle skier when she caught an edge in the world finals in Canada on April 11, 2015. Being the first woman to perform a double-flip in slopestyle skiing at the X Games in 2013, she had decided that, to win, she would push herself to perform an off-axis double backflip in the second run. Ranked either number one or number two in the world in her event for three years running, she had to push her boundaries and go for it.

Pushing boundaries was not new for Jamie. There is a backstory to her courageous spirit that enabled her to test the limits of her sport. Her last name says it all—her original surname isn't MoCrazy, but Crane-Mauzy. She made the change when she got married in 2022 because MoCrazy reflects who Jamie is.

You could say she was a crazy kid. MoCrazy became a childhood nickname that stuck, and it's apropos as it led her to a fearless career as a top skier. The nickname stemmed all the way back to when she was just a one-year-old. Jamie climbed the living room curtains and found herself stuck at the top, unable to climb back down. Her mother got to her before she fell and helped her get down. Later her mom would teach Jamie some important lessons, such as to think creatively in any challenging life situation, become self-reliant, and commit herself to finding a solution. That would become the foundation for Jamie's action plan—commit to a goal that requires a sequence of steps to push through any mental or physical challenges that came her way. And that approach to life got her to the top of the mountain.

But on that fateful day in April 2015, Jamie crashed. Her head slammed onto the hard snowpack, causing bleeding in her brain, damage to her brain stem, and paralysis on her right side.

Jamie awoke from a coma ten days later with the cognitive, motor, and behavioral skills of that one-year-old who had climbed the curtain twenty-one years earlier. It would take many years to recover, and depression ensued. That depression would have become severe if not for the strength and support of her family and the opportunity she had to start seeing a therapist. As Jamie describes it today, she had to embark on not only a physical recovery, but an invisible one as well.

The physical therapy demands were intense, and her emotional stability, which had been unquestionably strong prior to the accident, was now severely compromised as well. Her invisible recovery required that she relearn how to talk, to find words that were now hidden in a vault she could no longer tap into. Her cognition and emotions took a huge hit and would become her largest hurdle in life.

Then came the beginning of Jamie 2.0. She fought through her challenge one step at a time. She regained her motor skills, and her cognition returned to normal. She went back to college and got a degree in communications from Westminster University in Salt Lake City. In Jamie's words, her recovery allowed her to "go from ordinary to extraordinary through the process." She was on a mission to reinvent herself.

When she regained her physical abilities and began hiking again, she would sometimes need to stop and take a break, which was incredibly frustrating for a competitive skier who had climbed to the top of so many mountains. On one hike, her mother, a psychotherapist, told her that instead of saying she needed to "take a break," she should try saying, "look at the view." That concept would turn into a life metaphor for Jamie. "Looking at the view" meant reflecting on a daily basis to appreciate all that life has to offer.

Like me, Jamie credits her openness to finding inspiration from others to get her through the darkest days. Her mother's words helped her realize that life can alternate between peaks and valleys.

Today Jamie 2.0 is an incredible person. Her recovery from traumatic brain injury (TBI) helped her rediscover the sense of purpose she had in childhood. Her passion in childhood had been to help young girls in Third World countries to believe in themselves. Today, she and her family run the MoCrazy Strong Foundation, a charitable organization that raises awareness about TBI and provides educational services for "complementary mind-body medicine to create whole-body recoveries."[54]

Jamie's motivation and drive have sustained her at the forefront of her mission to climb alternative peaks, and as a motivational speaker Jamie inspires others to get back up from what may have knocked them down and climb their own mountains.

For more information and to contact Jamie MoCrazy, visit MoCrazyStrong.org.

---

54   Author interview with Jamie MoCrazy on February 21, 2024, and website content from http://www.mocrazystrong.org.

JASON SCHECHTERLE

J ason Schechterle always had dreams and achieved many of his goals by the age of twenty-eight. He served in the U.S. Air Force until he was twenty-six and then became a police officer in Phoenix, Arizona. He was a two handicap in golf. And like me before my cancer diagnosis, he was living on Easy Street. But just fourteen months into his new career as a police officer, everything changed.

Jason was en route to an emergency call in his patrol car on the evening of March 26, 2001, when a taxicab driver suffering an epileptic seizure shot through an intersection at 115 mph. The taxi rear-ended Jason after he had made a brief stop at a red light, trapping him inside his vehicle amidst a burst of flames.

Jason didn't wake up for two and a half months. He had burns over 40 percent of his body, including fourth-degree burns from the neck up. Jason awoke to discover he was completely blind, and his six-foot-three frame had shed sixty-one pounds. His appearance was severely altered, and he endured more than fifty surgical procedures. He lost half his fingers to amputation and was unable to talk.

Acceptance, Accountability, and Gratefulness

But there are blessings in every curse. As Jason describes it, the most difficult part of his adversity and the most beautiful blessing that resulted from it were the same thing—his blindness.

Had he been able to look in the mirror at the time of his accident, he doubts he could have handled it. And this is where reflection became a big part of how Jason coped with his adversity. Jason did not focus on self-pity, but rather used reflection as a force to build an action plan. That drive is a hallmark of resilience. Jason's plan focused on the following:

- Acceptance: He could not move forward without accepting what happened to him on that fateful day and deciding to face his challenges.
- Accountability: He had no one to blame. He was responsible for every choice he made in his life, including the route he chose and the intersection he was navigating that day.
- Gratefulness: His support team and the lessons he learned about life were his greatest gifts.

Acceptance. Accountability. Gratefulness. These would become key tenets in his life. As Jason says time and again, "Life is 10 percent what happens to us and 90 percent how we react to it."

Keep the Proper Perspective

Nine months after his accident, surgeons opened the skin grafts they had placed over Jason's eyes in an attempt to protect his corneas. The protective skin grafts were what had caused his blindness. Once released from the confinement of the grafts, Jason could see light and color again, but at the time, the acuteness of his vision was about on par with being underwater in a swimming pool with your eyes open, looking from one end to the other. His eyesight eventually returned to normal.

He endured physical therapy and speech therapy. He was starting life all over again. But Jason was determined. He blew every recovery timeline out of the water and was able to return home six months earlier than projected.

Grit and determination are one thing, but as you know from this book it is essential to have a community of support made up of family, friends, colleagues, and the medical professionals who work miracles. In addition, his positive attitude and abiding faith enabled him to remain hopeful, and he credits his support system, faith, and positivity with giving him the peace of mind to not sweat the small stuff and keep life in perspective.

Today, he is incredibly grateful and knows he can change the course of his toughest days by performing random acts of kindness for others. When he does things for others, he feels blessed and happy to be alive.

Jason and his wife are also grateful they were able to bring a third child into the world eighteen months after his accident. Two weeks after that, Jason drove himself back to the Phoenix Police Department to begin his new career as a homicide detective, another goal he had set for himself well before his accident. His incredible drive and goal achievement are truly an inspiration. He never settled for second best. He set out to achieve the goals he had before his accident and never believed they wouldn't be possible. He faced every challenge head-on. He took control. And despite losing half his fingers, he still cherishes the outlets he had before his accident. In fact, he is now a one handicap. I wish I could take golf lessons from Jason. Maybe one day I will.

Jason is prepared for any future adversity. His acceptance and gratefulness define his resilience. He and his wife attend Catholic church services every Sunday, and Jason finds that one hour in church each week is the opportunity for deep-dive reflection. He ponders what he did over the past week, right and wrong, and what he can do better next week.

I smiled when I heard him share his church story because it reminded me of my father, who attended mass every Sunday as well. I recall my dad bringing three-inch-by-five-inch index cards and a pen to mass with him every week. During the homily, he would pull out a card and write notes to himself. Perhaps they were epiphanies or inspirations, or perhaps just tasks he suddenly remembered he had to complete. I'll never know because I never asked. But it's likely his actions rubbed off on me and are one reason I found reflection to be so important in my own life.

Jason realized all his dreams, but his adversity helped him to focus on what his real calling became—to give back and share his experiences with audiences everywhere and inspire them to overcome their own challenges.

There is another silver lining in Jason's story that truly touched me. His daughter Kiley, who was just seven when Jason had his accident, also found a way to pay it forward with a newfound purpose that resulted from the experience. When she was only twelve, and after all she learned from Jason's ordeal, Kiley found her calling. She attended Baylor University's Developmental Child Psychology Program, and today she helps children affected by trauma. She learned a great deal at a young age, and we're all so lucky for her experience, passion, and life purpose.

In Jason's words, "Don't let the pain of today blind you from the promise of tomorrow."[55]

For more information and to contact Jason, visit BurningShield .com.

---

[55] Author interview with Jason Schechterle on March 11, 2024, and website content from http://www .burningshield.com.

The Potential Within to Win

Perseverance. Resilience. Courage. Hope. Empathy. That's what these stories of survival demonstrate. You too can overcome challenges and adversity if you push yourself to find courage. If you keep trying to find the silver lining under difficult circumstances. If you take some risks. And if you think positively and believe in yourself. Don't doubt what you can accomplish. Take one day at a time. Be purposeful with each day. Be intentional.

You too can bounce back from situations in ways you may never have thought possible.

My story and the stories of others in this book are just a small sample of the amazing things people can accomplish under difficult circumstances. You have read stories of tremendous courage and grace under pressure that are unique to each individual's experience with overcoming adversity. A main takeaway from these stories is that as we make progress toward a brighter future, we learn that life has more to offer us. Life gives us choices. We find a new purpose. For that, we can all be incredibly grateful.

May you too find the gifts that adversity inevitably delivers to us all. Be prepared. Find time to reflect. Don't be afraid to iterate and improve how you approach change. Find the courage and motivation to act each day. Life is a journey and a gift, so continue to optimize how you live.

Like many things in life, if you follow a proven process, results will follow. Not only can you overcome adversity, you can rebuild your self-confidence and improve your self-esteem, helping you find success, happiness, and purpose. The world is full of possibilities and surprises. Embrace them and thrive.

Acknowledgments

I am grateful to many, many people without whose support and encouragement this book would never have been possible.

First and foremost, I thank those who helped me during my battle with cancer and its aftermath. I am grateful that there were so many people who provided selfless support and positivity throughout my ordeal, especially my mother, father, three brothers, and my close friends.

I am grateful for my medical team, especially Dr. Roger Crumley, Dr. Ian Zlotolow, Dr. Ted Phillips, Carolyn Clary, Adrienne Low, and Claire Alexander. Without you, I wouldn't be here to tell the story. I will always honor you for going above and beyond the call of duty and being so committed to improved patient outcomes.

There were many key turning points in my life, and I am so appreciative of the people who made those possible. I thank Dina for her honesty, which changed the course of my life. I thank the Cancer Support Community as a whole—so many in the organization provided kindness, encouragement, and sincerity.

I want to thank my wife Sue, who has been my partner and supporter for over thirty years. Her encouragement and feedback throughout the writing of this book have been invaluable. I love you so much.

I wish to thank Tyler Higgins for his encouragement and belief in this book. He was there for me when I was battling my cancer and has remained a huge support to me in all the years since. His excitement when this book found a home meant the world to me.

To my dearest friend Tom Witter, who was with me throughout my ordeal, I thank you from the deepest place in my heart. Tom is the definition of a true friend.

In the editing of my manuscript, I want to thank Bonnie Hearn Hill, who made the time to work tirelessly on it despite her busy career as a successful author herself. She offered tremendous encouragement, and she believed in this book after reading just the first chapter. Thank you, Bonnie!

I wish to thank my literary agent, Marc Mikulich, for being a superb communicator and for his encouragement and belief in my manuscript. I thank everyone at ECW Press for believing in this book, especially Jennifer Smith. And I was so incredibly lucky to get to work with my primary editor, Don Loney, whose honesty, tact, and talent go unmatched. He was tireless in his commitment to making my manuscript the best it could be. Lastly, I am grateful to David Marsh, my copy editor, who so meticulously reviewed the manuscript and suggested critical clarifications to take it to the finish line.

Thank you to all those who took the time to review and endorse this book. And a huge thank-you to the heroes whose stories I share in the final chapter. You are my inspiration.

About the Author

A survivor of a permanent facial difference and life-threatening cancer, Terry Healey is an author, keynote speaker, and business consultant. Healey challenges audiences to face their adversities and to apply his framework of four key principles to gain confidence, build resilience, and find joy in their personal and professional lives.

Having endured more than thirty surgical procedures to reconstruct his face while in his early twenties, Healey discovered tools that could help him transform his changed life. He shares ways to take control, overcome challenges, build trust and teams, embrace change, and learn the value of acceptance and tolerance. He views the lessons he learned as gifts, and believes his greatest reward is being able to teach others how to overcome any kind of adversity and celebrate life.

His experience led him to a successful thirty-five-year career as a high-tech sales and marketing executive, including being on the founding team of a company that had a successful initial public offering. His popular programs are presented to healthcare organizations, corporations, educational institutions, associations, and nonprofits nationwide. They include Cisco Systems, Inc., Charles Schwab, the University of California Berkeley football team, Santa Clara University, Ligand Pharmaceuticals, Genomic Health, Perkin Elmer, Stanford University, UC San Francisco, Kaiser Permanente, Northwestern Memorial Hospital, Greater Baltimore Medical Center, Lawrence Livermore National Laboratory, and many others.

A graduate of UC Berkeley, Healey is the author of *At Face Value: My Triumph Over a Disfiguring Cancer*, and is a contributing author to *Open My Eyes, Open My Soul: Celebrating Our Common Humanity; Make Your Own Miracle: Surviving Cancer, an Anthology;* and *Reading Lips and Other Ways to Overcome a Disability.*

His work has appeared in *Psychology Today, Metro UK, The San Francisco Chronicle, Guideposts, NurseWeek, U.S. News and World Report, Sales and Marketing Magazine, Coping,* and *CURE Today.* He has appeared on dozens of national and local TV networks and has been interviewed on more than seventy-five radio stations across the U.S. and Canada.